What the Bible Says About Your Provision and Prosperity

Trevor Newport

New Wine Press

New Wine Press
PO Box 17
Chichester
West Sussex PO20 6YB
England

ISBN: 1 874367 82 5

Typeset by CRB Associates, Reepham, Norfolk
Printed in England by Clays Ltd, St Ives plc.

Contents

Chapter 1

Introduction to Prosperity

I have been a Christian now for nearly twenty years. When I first became a believer in Jesus Christ my life changed dramatically in many areas because I was so far away from any knowledge of spiritual things.

However, when I look back to that time in my life I realise that one particular attitude arose almost immediately which I did not recognise at all. Straight after my conversion to Christianity I decided to get rid of my good clothes and dress shabbily. I was engulfed with the feeling that Christians should not have anything at all because of all the people starving in the world and that it was a sin to buy new clothes – or new anything! It was amazing because before my conversion I never thought about that once.

What was going on? Why was I thinking like this? Was this a godly thought?

Anyway, this feeling went on for quite some time and nobody around me at the time gave me any teaching from the Word of God on the subject. Looking back at this time I can see exactly what was going on but it took me years to overcome in this vital area of doctrine.

It is all to do with upbringing. I was brought up in a very good home, for which I praise God. My parents cared for me and always tried their best for me. However, they had no knowledge of God or His Word in their lives and where finances were concerned I was brought up with the 'can't afford' mentality. My parents, in their ignorance, passed on a 'poverty spirit' to me. Of course it was not their fault and I do not hold anything against them for it at all. It also has to do with the way that **they** were brought up and the way that their parents were brought up before them. I was the victim of several generations of a poverty mentality which went deep into my heart and robbed me for the first few years of my Christian life.

The next thing which I remember vividly is my introduction to the teaching of prosperity. I was angry at the thought that we should be prospering when there were so many poor people in the world! I was blinded by the devil in this area of my life. As I listened to this well-known preacher, I would be agreeing with everything that he said about healing, victory, authority, peace and joy but as soon as he would speak about prosperity I would immediately have a change of countenance. This generational build-up of poverty in my life would rise up and challenge every word. I would like to be able to say that in a few short months I studied the Scriptures and this revelation came. However, I have to tell you the truth: I was bound. I could only accept that God would provide our basic needs. Consequently, I was always in need and needed a miracle because I was believing that way! You get what you believe for. It took years before I understood this subject.

If you are relating to all this then I ask you to persevere throughout this book until you have read what God has to say about this vital subject. His Truth will always find a way into our hearts if we are humble enough to take the time to seek His Word.

This subject will not go away! You will have to decide sooner or later. Take a close look at the following verses of Scripture and spend a few moments meditating on them:

> *'Let them shout for joy, and be glad, that favour my righteous cause: yea, let them say continually, Let the Lord be magnified, which hath pleasure in the prosperity of his servant.'*   (Psalm 35:27)

> *'But thou shalt remember the* Lord *thy God: for it is he that giveth thee power to get wealth, that he may establish his covenant which he sware unto thy fathers, as it is this day.'*
> (Deuteronomy 8:18)

'And all these blessings shall come on thee, and overtake thee, if thou shalt hearken unto the voice of the LORD thy God.'
(Deuteronomy 28:2)

'A good man leaveth an inheritance to his children's children: and the wealth of the sinner is laid up for the just.'
(Proverbs 13:22)

'Beloved, I wish above all things that thou mayest prosper and be in health, even as thy soul prospereth.' (3 John 2)

*'But my God shall supply all your need **according to his riches in glory by Christ Jesus.'*** (Philippians 4:19)

It took me about ten years before I realised what Philippians 4:19 meant! This verse does not say that God will provide for your need. God's provision for us is not determined by the size of our need. He does not provide for our need **according to our need**. Instead, He provides for our need **according to His riches in glory by Christ Jesus**!

You will also notice from 3 John 2 that we only prosper financially and experience health when our soul is prospering! Health and wealth are directly proportional to our soul being right with God and to seeking His face, coupled with absolute obedience to His will!

I challenge you to read all the way through this book and to study the Scriptures carefully before you make any final conclusions about this life-changing subject.

For those of you who believe the Bible already about prosperity, my prayer is that you will grow in your understanding and revelation knowledge to become a blessing towards God's work, to reach people for Christ and also to bless the poor both financially and spiritually.

Chapter 2

A Revelation of Prosperity

As we go on in the Christian life we never stop learning. Or should I say we should never stop learning! I am not referring just to head knowledge but particularly to **revelation knowledge**. Even things that we have known about for years can become fresh revelation under a special anointing from God.

Look at what Isaiah says:

> *'For precept must be upon precept, precept upon precept; line upon line, line upon line; here a little, and there a little.'*
>
> (Isaiah 28:10)

I have learned over the years that we do not learn everything from just one source of ministry. Sometimes you learn much from one ministry and a little from someone else and vice versa. The Pharisees were unteachable and we must always guard ourselves against thinking that we know it all.

What is prosperity?

The world operates on a mentality of 'How can I get?' Prosperity in the kingdom of God says the opposite: 'How can I *give*?'

The word *'blessed'* means 'empowered to prosper' according to one translation. One of the things that the Lord is always saying to His obedient, faithful, holy people is that He wants to bless us all through Scripture. Thus He wants to prosper us.

'If ye be willing and obedient, ye shall eat the good of the land.' (Isaiah 1:19)

'And it shall come to pass, if thou shalt hearken diligently unto the voice of the LORD thy God, to observe and to do all his commandments which I command thee this day, that the LORD thy God will set thee on high above all nations of the earth: And all these blessings shall come on thee, and overtake thee, if thou shalt hearken unto the voice of the LORD thy God. Blessed shalt thou be in the city, and blessed shalt thou be in the field.' (Deuteronomy 28:1–3)

If you read the whole of this chapter you will see what God promised for His people if they were obedient to Him in all things. You will also see what God said would happen if they were not obedient! Therefore, we can read from this passage that prosperity means to be blessed in every area of life.

What is prosperity for?

Prosperity is certainly not for us to sit back and watch the world go by while we fulfil the lusts of the flesh on ourselves! The Bible tells us that God wants to bless us so that we can be a blessing. How can we help someone else if we do not have enough for ourselves? Someone who has no resources would like to help the poor but becomes frustrated because he can **do nothing about it**.

The other reason for prosperity is to promote the kingdom of God – which costs money.

'But thou shalt remember the LORD thy God: for it is he that giveth thee power to get wealth, that he may establish his covenant which he sware unto thy fathers, as it is this day.' (Deuteronomy 8:18)

This verse puts everything into perspective! If you are a Christian and God has made you wealthy it is for the purpose of establishing **His** covenant in the Earth. Of course it means the New Covenant now. You can see now why this subject has been criticised so much by so many religious-minded people. The devil wants to stop the preaching of the

Gospel. How does he do it? If he can sow a poverty spirit into Christians then he has won a major battle against the army of God because no army can go to battle without resources. Things cost money. Churches cost money, book publication costs money, missionary work costs money – in fact everything to do with the Gospel costs money. All Satan has to do is to stop people giving into the kingdom of God and he has won two victories!

Firstly, the individual will stop being blessed and secondly the work of the ministry will slow down apart from the miraculous power of God. People have tried to co-operate with the devil in not supporting our ministry but God always shows up with a miracle anyway and is not bound by people's disobedience. People do not control ministries. God is our source! Praise His Name! If you are controlled by a poverty spirit then you must declare war against it by speaking out the Word of God concerning finances. You also need to renounce and repent of a poverty spirit and command it never to dictate to you again in the financial realm. The Lord wants to bless you so that you can be a constant blessing.

What is a poverty spirit?

The Bible says that we can only have one master, namely God:

> *'No man can serve two masters: for either he will hate the one, and love the other; or else he will hold to the one, and despise the other. Ye cannot serve God and mammon.'*
>
> (Matthew 6:24)

Who is your God? Those who do not support the Gospel have answered this question before all the holy angels. A poverty spirit is the most selfish and ungodly characteristic which squeezes the life out of its victim. You co-operate with it every time you refuse to give generously into the work of God. If you say that God is your master then prove it by becoming liberal in your giving. People who do not give are declaring that money is their God.

'For the love of money is the root of all evil: which while some coveted after, they have erred from the faith, and pierced themselves through with many sorrows.'

(1 Timothy 6:10)

This verse does not say that money but the **love** of money is evil. It also warns against covetousness. Having money does not make you covetous. It is usually the other way around. Those who do not have money are usually the ones who commit crimes involving money!

The way to avoid covetousness is to become generous in giving and to look for ways to give and support the work of God, feeding the poor etc.

The Bible warns us against seeking earthly treasures and the things of this life.

'But seek ye first the kingdom of God, and his righteousness; and all these things shall be added unto you.'

(Matthew 6:33)

If we continually seek Him first in our lives and take care of His business then all the things that we need for this life should take care of themselves.

Prosperity for the whole man

When we talk about prosperity from the Scriptures we do not just mean in the financial realm, although that is the main focus of attention of this particular book. Biblical prosperity means body, soul and spirit. It includes healing, peace of mind, victory over Satan, blessed children, a sound mind, protection, deliverance etc. The word of God has provided prosperity in every area of life, not just for finances. A man can become extremely rich with money but die of incurable diseases. That is not real prosperity, is it? In fact some of the world's richest men have died that way. My prayer for you is that you prosper in every area of your life so that you can fulfil your ultimate calling on earth and be a blessing to multitudes!

Chapter 3

Atonement Prosperity

'For ye know the grace of our Lord Jesus Christ, that, though he was rich, yet for your sakes he became poor, that ye through his poverty might be rich.'　　(2 Corinthians 8:9)

When was Jesus made poor? I used to think that this meant during His earthly life. After all, there was no room in the Inn, and the Son of man had nowhere to lay His head. Jesus Himself said;

'And Jesus looked round about, and saith unto his disciples, How hardly shall they that have riches enter into the kingdom of God! And the disciples were astonished at his words. But Jesus answereth again, and saith unto them, Children, how hard is it for them that trust in riches to enter into the kingdom of God! It is easier for a camel to go through the eye of a needle, than for a rich man to enter into the kingdom of God. And they were astonished out of measure, saying among themselves, Who then can be saved?'

(Mark 10:23–26)

Jesus is warning His disciples here about trusting in riches because they were so rich themselves. Look at verse 26! *'Who then can be saved?'* This statement could only mean that all of the disciples of Jesus were wealthy!

There are some highly respected Bible teachers in the world today who teach that Jesus Himself owned His own house, taking Mark 2:1 as a supporting Scripture. Another translation says, *'he was at home'*. Others claim that Jesus

was referring to Peter's house. I personally do not think that
there is enough evidence to prove either way.

Jews were not poor in those days and neither are they
today despite what some people have tried to do to them.
Therefore the only conclusion that we can come to regarding 2 Corinthians 8:9 is that **Jesus took our poverty on the
Cross**, along with all the other negative things that Adam
gained when he fell. Jesus was made poor on the Cross to
pay the price for our poverty to deliver us from it. You are
rich because of what He did – **not just spiritually but
financially as well**! This verse has changed my whole
attitude to the subject of finances. I have decided to become
a 'reservoir' to be able to direct money into the preaching of
the Gospel etc.

Let me ask you a question: who would you prefer to be
controlling this world's resources? Those involved in porno-
graphy, drug pushers, Freemasons – or those reaching out to
the lost and poor? I would rather that money was spent
wisely for the sake of the Kingdom above anything else in
the world. Agree with me now for a major transfer of money
from the sinful world into the Kingdom of God.

1. Jesus took my sin to make me righteous (2 Corinthians
   5:21).
2. Jesus bore my sickness and carried my disease to give
   me healing (Matthew 8:17; 1 Peter 2:24).
3. Jesus was made poor to make me rich (2 Corinthians
   8:9).
4. Jesus was oppressed to deliver me (Isaiah 53:7).
5. Jesus went into hell to overcome Satan to give me
   victory (Acts 2).

Consequently, when Jesus was on the Cross He bore my
poverty and made me rich instead. All I have to do is **simply
to believe it**. This is why Peter says,

> '*According as **his divine power hath given unto us all
> things that pertain unto life** and godliness, through the
> knowledge of him that hath called us to glory and virtue.'*
> (2 Peter 1:3)

The day you were born again you received everything that
God has for you in His Word. We already have all things

that pertain to this life! Jesus has delivered me from poverty and lack once and for all and blessed me so that I can be a blessing to others, look after my family and support the Gospel. However, having said that, this does not give you a license to go and write cheques from your bank account when there is no money in it! Make sure that you read all the chapters in this book and take heed to all the Scriptures relevant to prosperity. Many people have made bad mistakes which have cost them years of their life because they have heard just enough to get themselves into trouble. Unfortunately there are many who try to operate at a higher level in the financial realm without taking all the necessary steps that the Lord determines.

I once heard someone make a very interesting statement about money:

'Money takes on the personality of the person using it.'

I had never thought of that before. It is true. Think for a moment about £20 in the hand of a drug-user. That money would probably go to buy £20 worth of drugs. Put that same £20 into the hand of a gambler and it would be used on something else equally destructive. But if you put that same £20 into the hand of a single mother, she would use it to feed or clothe her children. The £20 has no say in the matter. You do not know who handled your present hard currency before you. It could have been used for anything. Once you are the legal owner of that money it does not matter what it was used for before. It is now in your power to do with it whatever you wish!

Therefore, money itself is not evil at all. It is simply a servant to the person who controls it.

Chapter 4

Opening the Windows of Heaven

The Lord decided a long time ago to introduce a system into His work that would bless the giver and God's work. It is a simple principle which my wife and I have been following for nearly two decades. Study the following Scriptures carefully:

> 'And blessed be the most high God, which hath delivered thine enemies into thy hand. And he gave him tithes of all.'
> (Genesis 14:20)

> 'But the tithes of the children of Israel, which they offer as an heave offering unto the LORD, I have given to the Levites to inherit: therefore I have said unto them, Among the children of Israel they shall have no inheritance.'
> (Numbers 18:24).

> 'Will a man rob God? Yet ye have robbed me. But ye say, Wherein have we robbed thee? In tithes and offerings … Bring ye all the tithes into the storehouse, that there may be meat in mine house, and prove me now herewith, saith the LORD of hosts, if I will not open you the windows of heaven, and pour you out a blessing, that there shall not be room enough to receive it.'
> (Malachi 3:8, 10)

> 'And verily they that are of the sons of Levi, who receive the office of the priesthood, have a commandment to take tithes of the people according to the law, that is, of their brethren, though they come out of the loins of Abraham: But he whose descent is not counted from them received tithes of Abraham,

*and blessed him that had the promises ... And here men
that die receive tithes; but there he receiveth them, of whom
it is witnessed that he liveth. And as I may so say, Levi also,
who receiveth tithes, payed tithes in Abraham.'*

(Hebrews 7:5–6, 8–9)

Tithing is God's way of financing His work on Earth along
with offerings.

What does *'tithing'* mean?

The **tithe** simply means 'a tenth' or ten percent of our total
income or any other money we receive. Ruth and I give a
tenth, to begin with, of all our income including gifts,
inheritances, lump sums and any other money that comes
our way.

Where do we give our tithe?

The verses that we have quoted from Malachi in this chapter
say that all the tithes must be brought into the 'storehouse'
so that there is 'meat in mine house'. Therefore the storehouse can only be referring to God's house which today
means the local church. Thus all of our tithes should go into
the storehouse. We never even consider giving our tithe to
any other ministry or preacher or anybody. It belongs in the
local church always.

**This opens the windows of heaven upon you financ-
ially and in other ways**. These open windows are obviously
kept open by consistently tithing 52 weeks of the year. True
discipleship involves tithing. I do not hesitate to say that
anyone who is not tithing is not yet a true disciple of Jesus
Christ. We all have to pay income tax if we are earning
money and look what Jesus said:

*'And Jesus answering said unto them, Render to Caesar the
things that are Caesar's, and to God the things that are
God's. And they marvelled at him.'*   (Mark 12:17)

Most of us pay our income tax without even questioning
it. How much more should we pay our tithes! God is giving

us an opportunity to prove Him in finances. I can testify that in all the time that I have been tithing God has **never failed me once**. And for the first 12 years of ministry my wife and I had to have a financial miracle every month during that time since my salary was so small. We always gave our tithes and offerings (I will talk about offerings later) even when it meant needing a miracle to see us through. We have received literally hundreds of financial miracles of provision without telling anyone about our needs.

I was in a hotel room in Argentina in February of 1997 without a credit card and no means of getting any money from anywhere. I was staying in a three-star hotel in Beunos Aires and preaching most days. In two days time I would have to pay the hotel bill and I had very little money left in my pocket. The telephone rang and the secretary of the church that I was with told me that there was no money to give me for an offering. I said nothing about my situation and told her not to worry about me. I did not even think about how God was going to find the £400 pounds in 36 hours. I was in the will of God. He had told me to go to Argentina so I knew that He would provide.

Two hours later the telephone in my hotel room rang again and two lovely people wanted to see me to ask for some advice. They came to the hotel and we talked. I said absolutely nothing about my need since if I tell people what the need is I rule God out of the picture. I wanted the need met according to His riches in glory by Christ Jesus. This precious gentleman then handed me an envelope and told me that God had told him to pay my airfare (he did not know how much it was). He gave me $1030 which was the price of it almost exactly! He then paid cash for some Life-Changing Ministries books.

That night I went to another church and they gave another $300, and the previous church (the one that had told me they had no money), gave me another $600. I was then able to pay the hotel bill and cover the entire trip as well as blessing Life-Changing Ministries back home with book sales. God never fails.

When we first started trusting God for money it used to be small amounts of £10 and then £20. I remember one night

I went out to a meeting and left my wife Ruth in to look after our two babies. We had no money left and had just eaten our last meal. I told nobody about our situation and while I was out at the meeting somebody handed me an envelope which had 'anonymous' written on the front. I opened it and found one note inside. It was a £50 note! I had never seen one before and we had never seen that size gift before. (This was sixteen years ago when £50 was a lot of money.) Then, a few weeks later, we had our first £100 breakthrough and have had many since. The Lord has always provided for us because we tithe. Hallelujah!

The Lord has moved us on in this realm to the point where our projects in the financial realm are five, six and seven figures. The Lord gave me a huge challenge in 1996 to believe Him for something that will cost about £4,000,000 along with all our other projects.

> *'Though thy beginning was small, yet thy latter end should greatly increase.'*   (Job 8:7)

> *'For who hath despised the day of small things? for they shall rejoice, and shall see the plummet in the hand of Zerubbabel with those seven; they are the eyes of the LORD, which run to and fro through the whole earth.'*
>   (Zechariah 4:10)

The Lord usually starts us off in the small things and looks for faithfulness before big things can be entrusted to us. If we are faithful in little God will one day make us ruler over much.

> *'His lord said unto him, Well done, thou good and faithful servant: thou hast been faithful over a few things, I will make thee ruler over many things: enter thou into the joy of thy lord.'*   (Matthew 25:21)

> *'The steps of a good man are ordered by the LORD: and he delighteth in his way.'*   (Psalm 37:23)

Take all of the steps that He gives you and the steps will become larger and larger.

Chapter 5

Offerings Above the Tithe

'For where your treasure is, there will your heart be also.'
(Matthew 6:21)

Let us look at the passage in Malachi fully.

'Will a man rob God? Yet ye have robbed me. But ye say, Wherein have we robbed thee? In tithes and offerings. Ye are cursed with a curse: for ye have robbed me, even this whole nation. Bring ye all the tithes into the storehouse, that there may be meat in mine house, and prove me now herewith, saith the LORD of hosts, if I will not open you the windows of heaven, and pour you out a blessing, that there shall not be room enough to receive it. And I will rebuke the devourer for your sakes, and he shall not destroy the fruits of your ground; neither shall your vine cast her fruit before the time in the field, saith the LORD of hosts. And all nations shall call you blessed: for ye shall be a delightsome land, saith the LORD of hosts.'
(Malachi 3:8–12)

In verse 11 we are told that the devourer will be rebuked by God Himself once we have given our tithes and then all nations will be affected through us. All because of tithing into His house! Our ministry has only been in existence for less than six years at the time of writing and from humble beginnings in our little home we now have a ministry in all six continents. Our books have gone into 29 countries in five different languages. I have been to 27 countries in the last four years to minister the Gospel. Praise God!

Tithing therefore opens the windows so that the Gospel can be preached all over the world. Once the windows are open through tithing we then come to offerings on top of the tithe. In the Old Testament the people of God brought all kinds of offerings as well as the tithes into the house of the Lord: wave offerings, heave offerings, sin offerings, thanksgiving offerings, peace offerings etc.

Today we can always give a thanksgiving offering to the Lord anytime we want to. Also there are times when a church needs to buy something and so a specific offering is taken up. This would constitute an offering over our tithe. In our church we teach our people to bring their tithes generally on a Sunday and then an offering on a Thursday at our midweek service. As Spirit-filled believers we need to listen to the voice of the Holy Spirit about what to give to God at offering times.

The law of multiplication

> *'But this I say, He which soweth sparingly shall reap also sparingly; and he which soweth bountifully shall reap also bountifully. **Every man according as he purposeth in his heart, so let him give; not grudgingly, or of necessity:** for God loveth a cheerful giver. And God is able to make all grace abound toward you; that ye, always having all sufficiency in all things, may abound to every good work: (As it is written, He hath dispersed abroad; he hath given to the poor: his righteousness remaineth for ever. Now he that ministereth seed to the sower both minister bread for your food, and multiply your seed sown, and increase the fruits of your righteousness;) Being enriched in every thing to all bountifulness, which causeth through us thanksgiving to God.'*   (2 Corinthians 9:6–11)

Verse 10 above promises us that our seed will multiply when sown in good ground with a joyful heart. Here is the Greek definition for the word *'cheerful'* in verse seven: *'hilaros'*: propitious or merry ('hilarious'), i.e. prompt or willing. So it actually can mean that we should be giving **hilariously**. The next time you give your offerings to God, do it hilariously. It is scriptural. I believe that this is included in the Word of God because it often takes great faith to give our offerings to God. By laughing about it we are declaring by faith that He will multiply it back to us which must make the devil very angry!

Satan is the thief who wants to stop you prospering. If the devil ever tries to tell you not to give to God in the offering then here is some advice for you. **Give more and start laughing**. It works! You can never outgive God. My wife and I have consistently increased the percentage amount that we give. Last year we gave 33 percent of our entire income to the Lord and we keep prospering! One man started by tithing and was blessed so he gave 20 percent and was even more blessed so he gave 30 percent until eventually he now gives 90 percent to the Lord and lives off the 10 percent! He has become a millionaire during that time.

Only God can do this! Why not prove Him for yourself?

Where should our offerings go?

Just as the children of Israel brought all of their offerings into the house of God, so should we. Ruth and I are extremely rich towards the house of God. We give all our tithes, offerings and seeds into our church. We also do things behind the scenes for the church that nobody sees.

The only time when we give an offering to another ministry is when God specifically tells us to, which we do from time to time.

The other kind of offering that we make is when we find out that someone is in need within the church firstly. This goes on all the time. We are always looking for ways to give.

You may have picked this book up thinking that you were going to get rich quick without **you** having to do anything about it! There is no such thing.

> *'Be not deceived; God is not mocked: for whatsoever a man soweth, that shall he also reap.'*   (Galatians 6:7)

If you sow nothing that is what you will get – nothing!

> *'Cast thy bread upon the waters: for thou shalt find it after many days.'*   (Ecclesiastes 11:1)

It is none of our business how or when it comes back to us. In this respect God usually surprises us. There are times when we have given some money away to someone and seen a harvest almost immediately.

Let me share a testimony. I once went to a ministers' meeting and I was just getting to know the voice of the Lord. In my wallet I had two £5 notes which Ruth was going to use for shopping when I arrived home since we had no food in the house. During the meeting the Holy Spirit spoke to me and said, 'Give John £5.' I reached into my wallet and took out £5 and gave it to him. He told me afterwards that he and his wife had no money either and so we both rejoiced.

When I arrived home within one hour of giving £5 to my friend I was given a cheque for £100! This is twenty times what I had just given away. It pays to obey. This is not an exception in my life but the norm. Ruth and I have lived like this for many years.

However, there are some times when we give an offering and it does not seem as if it multiplies at all. That is where faith comes in. I have sown thousands of offerings over the years and I believe that they are in good ground being prepared to be harvested for me. My seeds are multiplying and coming back to me. God has promised it to me and I believe it.

Some seeds take time just like some natural seeds on a farm. Some seeds grow up faster than others. So it is when we sow our financial seeds. The secret is to keep sowing and watering your seeds by confessing with your mouth that it is working.

Chapter 6

Debt and Borrowing Money

Take a close look at the following Scriptures and meditate on them for a while.

> 'The rich ruleth over the poor, and **the borrower is servant to the lender.'** (Proverbs 22:7)

> 'The LORD shall open unto thee his good treasure, the heaven to give the rain unto thy land in his season, and to bless all the work of thine hand: and thou shalt lend unto many nations, and thou shalt not borrow. **And the LORD shall make thee the head, and not the tail;** and thou shalt be above only, and thou shalt not be beneath; if that thou hearken unto the commandments of the LORD thy God, which I command thee this day, to observe and to do them.' (Deuteronomy 28:12–13)

> **'Owe no man any thing,** but to love one another: for he that loveth another hath fulfilled the law.' (Romans 13:8)

Over the years I have become more convinced about this subject of borrowing which will challenge many. The above Scriptures are very clear about living completely free of all debt. These verses say to me that every time I borrow money I become the tail instead of the head. God wants us as believers to be the head and not the tail! The verse in Proverbs says that the borrower is servant to the lender. This says to me that every time you borrow money you are ruling God out of your finances and making a declaration that He cannot provide for you. How do you think the Lord feels about that? It is a total lack of trust in God as your absolute source.

When it comes to the work of the Lord and you have a project involving huge sums of money, say a building for instance, it might look impossible without borrowing money to obtain it. However, I believe that every time you borrow money like this, even though it looks like you are moving forwards, you are actually going backwards! Firstly, borrowing money from almost all sources involves interest which means that you will end up paying far more for it than it is worth. This is true for everything. It also means that you are behind all the time instead of ahead. There is a better way which we have proved works every time without ever borrowing a penny. I also believe that Satan becomes involved in your finances because you have gone in the opposite direction to the Word of God. It is unbelief which needs to be repented of!

We are living in a society riddled with debt. Young couples are told to take out a mortgage as soon as possible and get into debt immediately. It sounds like good worldly advice because of the tax relief **but nobody ever tells them that they will end up paying up to three times the value of the property**!

My bank sends me letters almost every week trying to get me to borrow money. Credit card companies are always trying to get me to take out the next card. I do not use credit cards for anything by the way. I am completely free of all debt and everything in my house is paid for. I do not borrow money from any source whatsoever and will never need to. I have found a source that always gives me money as and when I need it. His Name is **Jehovah Jireh**, the Lord My Provider! He owns the cattle on a thousand hills. He can always bring meal in the barrel and oil in the cruse even in the worst famine. God is not controlled by the economy of the world (Genesis 22:14; Psalm 50:10; 1 Kings 17:12–16).

> *'But my God shall supply all your need according to his riches in glory by Christ Jesus.'*   (Philippians 4:19)

When are we as serious believers going to put our total and complete trust in God?

If you have been caught up in the world's system of debt and borrowed money I challenge you right now to repent and make a quality decision to trust the Lord from this day forward to provide everything for this life, and prosper. Some of you are probably disagreeing with me right now and saying that God provides through banks etc. Read the above Scriptures again and see what His Word says. I believe that many of you would be much further on in life in your personal lives and the work of the Lord if you had not borrowed at all.

Later on in this book we shall be looking at how to see big projects in the financial realm.

If you are in debt then you must make that a top priority first before you start on another project.

How to get out of debt

1. Repent of getting into debt and ask God to forgive you.
2. Make a decision not to borrow again for anything.
3. Continue giving your tithes into the local church.
4. Sow a particular seed for each debt that you have.
5. Pray in faith for the money to come as Jesus taught in Mark 11:22–24.
6. Name your seed for that debt. Be specific. If you owe £1000 then give £10 into your church and believe for a hundred-fold return which makes £1000.
7. Once the seed is in the ground do not dig it up by saying it is not working! Keep praising God for the money and in time it will be there.

We shall be looking at naming our seed and the hundred-fold return later in the book.

I want to share a testimony with you that will encourage you. Ruth and I were in debt many years ago and we decided to clear all of our debts. We owed several thousand pounds which was crippling us financially. We made a decision that as soon as we were paid each month that we would pay our tithes and offerings and regular bills (not food, petrol or anything else) and pay our debts with the rest. We did this for six and half months! We did not go to the shops for anything except milk and bread. We were desperate to clear our debts so that we could live properly. During that time we saw so many miracles come our way. People brought us food parcels, we were given money some weeks, someone even brought us a cooked meal every day for a whole week. We told nobody about our situation. At the end of this time we were totally free of debt. The Lord then spoke to my heart and said this:

'Because you have believed my word absolutely regarding finances you will now go first class for me.'

Since that time we have been so blessed in so many areas. I have just been all the way to Australia and back and travelled in Business Class. I keep being put up classes when I travel on airlines for no reason. My wife and I were coming home from California with our children from our annual holiday and Ruth and I were put up to First Class all the way to New York: a ticket that would have cost at least £1000 each extra!

What about mortgages?

Whichever way you look at a mortgage for a house or anything it is always borrowed money. Your house does not belong to you until you have paid the very last payment! It is on loan to you from the lender. You will end up paying between two and a half and three times the value of it.

Is there another way?

How do we get a roof over our heads without borrowing? The simple way is to rent. Paul the apostle did!

'And Paul dwelt two whole years in his own hired house, and received all that came in unto him.'   (Acts 28:30)

Ruth and I have rented for a few years now while we are in faith for our own house to manifest. I know a man of God who prayed with his wife in agreement for a house and six years later they moved into a house and found out that six years previously to the day the house had its first brick laid in the foundation! That house soon became their house after a short period of renting it and it was paid for in cash. I went to preach in Escondido in Southern California one night and after the service the pastor told me that the previous year he and his wife had been in faith for their own house and one day God told him to go and choose the house of his dreams. He did and a few weeks later a man came into his church and gave the pastor the cash to buy his own house which was the same as the house he had chosen. This works!

Ruth and I were renting a small house one day and the landlady telephoned me and wanted to put up the rent. The following day two of our friends phoned me and asked me if I wanted to rent their house for the next few years. It was the house of my dreams (at the time) and also in the exact location where we wanted to live. A few years later I was praying one afternoon on my bed and I had an open vision. In the vision I saw a house and I knew exactly where it was and the Lord spoke and told me that this would become our house one day. I told Ruth and we went to look at it. It is the exact house that I have subconsciously always wanted. God has confirmed to all four of the Newports that this is our house. In the meantime we continue to rent.

We have just moved out of our other house and into a larger and newer house which is much closer to church. God is promoting us one step at a time. And we are patient to see our house paid for in full without a mortgage. I am determined to believe every word of God in every area of my life and see success continually.

We are the head and not the tail and I intend keeping it that way!

Chapter 7

Faith for Finances

'Now faith is the substance of things hoped for, the evidence of things not seen.' (Hebrews 11:1)

*'But **without faith it is impossible to please him**: for he that cometh to God must believe that he is, and that he is a rewarder of them that diligently seek him.'*

(Hebrews 11:6)

*'And Jesus answering saith unto them, Have faith in God. For verily I say unto you, That whosoever shall say unto this mountain, Be thou removed, and be thou cast into the sea; and shall not doubt in his heart, but shall believe that those things which he saith shall come to pass; he shall have whatsoever he saith. **Therefore I say unto you, What things soever ye desire, when ye pray, believe that ye receive them, and ye shall have them.***'*

(Mark 11:22–24)

Notice that this verse says *'What things soever ye desire,'* which means that the Lord has given us the absolute responsibility to ask for things that will glorify Him. If our hearts are right with God then we will be asking for the right things. The Word of God does not give us an exhaustive list of things to pray for but rather general principles such as;

*'**Ye ask, and receive not, because ye ask amiss, that ye may consume it upon your lusts.***'* (James 4:3)

> *'And whatsoever we ask, we receive of him, because we*
> *keep his commandments, and do those things that are*
> *pleasing in his sight.'*   (1 John 3:22)

These two verses alone ought to straighten out our
motives before asking for anything! The reason why some
people do not prosper is usually because of a violation of
these two verses. Check your own heart now. Are you asking
for things in the financial realm to consume upon your own
lusts? Are you in obedience to the will of God and doing
those things that are pleasing in His sight? If so then you
can ask in faith for your needs to be met according to His
riches in glory by Christ Jesus.

Double-mindedness

Faith only works when we are absolutely consistent about it:

> *'If any of you lack wisdom, **let him ask of God**, that giveth*
> *to all men liberally, and upbraideth not; **and it shall be***
> ***given him. But let him ask in faith, nothing wavering.***
> *For he that wavereth is like a wave of the sea driven with the*
> *wind and tossed. For **let not that man think that he***
> ***shall receive any thing of the Lord. A double minded***
> ***man is unstable in all his ways.'***   (James 1:5–8)

James uses an example of how to ask for wisdom by
remaining consistent and unwavering in faith and then
makes a general statement for receiving anything from the
Lord in verse 7. You have to be single-minded in your faith
in God to see results.

How to be consistent in faith

> *'Let us hold fast the profession of [our] faith without*
> *wavering; (for he is faithful that promised).'*
>
> (Hebrews 10:23)

The word 'our' in the above verse is in italics in the King
James Version, which means that it does not actually appear

in the Greek but was added later by the translators. This verse should therefore read;

> *'Let us hold fast the profession of **faith** without wavering;*
> *(for he is faithful that promised).'*   (Hebrews 10:23)

The word for 'profession' can be equally translated as 'confession' as the Greek for this is *'homologia'* which according to the Strong's Concordance means 'acknowledgement, confession or profession'.

Thus we have to hold fast the **confession of faith** without wavering to see maximum results. The Lord told Abraham a long time ago to confess what he believed about the promise of a son. Take a look at Paul's account of this adventure in faith.

> *'(As it is written, **I have made thee a father of many nations**,) before him whom he believed, even God, who quickeneth the dead, and **calleth those things which be not as though they were**. Who against hope believed in hope, that he might become the father of many nations, according to that which was spoken, So shall thy seed be. And **being not weak in faith, he considered not** his own body now dead, when he was about an hundred years old, neither yet the deadness of Sara's womb: **He staggered not at the promise of God through unbelief**; but **was strong in faith, giving glory to God**; And being fully persuaded that, what he had promised, he was able also to perform.'*
>   (Romans 4:17–21)

Abraham had to confess for decades before he saw Isaac! He was faced with probably the ultimate hurdle. Sarah had been barren all through her life and could never conceive. She was now well past the time of life when babies were possible naturally speaking. God told Abraham that he would surely have a son by Sarah. This was real faith. Abraham had to call those things which be not as though they were.

Not only did Abraham have to believe that God was able but also **that He would**! This same principle has to be adopted every time we pray in faith for finances for ourself or for God's work. I have to pray regularly for sums of money beyond my natural ability to provide for to do the work that God has called me to. At the moment I have to believe God for five or six trips abroad every year which costs thousands of pounds.

In the last year or so we have had to find £10,000 to pay for our book publications, all by faith. Each time God has told me to write a book I have never had the money to publish it. By the time the book is finished and ready for publication the money always comes! This is often how faith works. However, we never presume about finances. I never order anything that we cannot pay for. We wait until the money comes in. Anything else is presumption. I have seen ministries operating in huge debt simply because they do not wait for His perfect time. That is how we stay ahead all the time. The Lord's timing is always perfect!

I must say one thing here about faith for finances which many seem to miss. God will only pay for His projects. He only pays for what He orders. He does not pay for your ideas however good they may sound. Look at what Jesus says;

> *'Abide in me, and I in you. As the branch cannot bear fruit of itself, except it abide in the vine; no more can ye, except ye abide in me. I am the vine, ye are the branches: He that abideth in me, and I in him, the same bringeth forth much fruit:* **for without me ye can do nothing.** *If a man abide not in me, he is cast forth as a branch, and is withered; and men gather them, and cast them into the fire, and they are burned. If ye abide in me, and my words abide in you, ye shall ask what ye will, and it shall be done unto you. Herein is my Father glorified, that ye bear much fruit; so shall ye be my disciples.'*   (John 15:4–8)

Thus we are only servants of His instructions. My job is simply to listen to the Father's instructions and to carry them out. Then I know that He will pay for it. The following verses have helped me very much in this area:

> *'Behold, in this thou art not just: I will answer thee, that God is greater than man. Why dost thou strive against him? for he giveth not account of any of his matters. For God speaketh once, yea twice, yet man perceiveth it not. In a*

dream, in a vision of the night, when deep sleep falleth upon men, in slumberings upon the bed; **Then he openeth the ears of men, and sealeth their instruction, That he may withdraw man from his purpose, and hide pride from man.'** (Job 33:12–17)

Therefore the most important thing in our life is to develop a close, personal and intimate relationship with the Lord and seek His face so that we can always hear accurately what He tells us. We can then move out in confidence knowing that He will bring in all the finances. (See Psalm 27:8.)

'So then faith cometh by hearing, and hearing by the word of God.' (Romans 10:17)

Fill your life with the Word of God and strong faith will be produced.

'But be ye doers of the word, and not hearers only, deceiving your own selves.' (James 1:22)

Chapter 8

The Hundredfold Return

*'Then Isaac sowed in that land, and received in the same year an **hundredfold**: and the L*ORD* blessed him.'*

(Genesis 26:12)

*'But other fell into good ground, and brought forth fruit, some an **hundredfold**, some sixtyfold, some thirtyfold.'*

(Matthew 13:8)

*'But he that received seed into the good ground is he that heareth the word, and understandeth it; which also beareth fruit, and bringeth forth, some an **hundredfold**, some sixty, some thirty.'*

(Matthew 13:23)

*'And every one that hath forsaken houses, or brethren, or sisters, or father, or mother, or wife, or children, or lands, for my name's sake, shall receive an **hundredfold**, and shall inherit everlasting life.'*

(Matthew 19:29)

*'But he shall receive an **hundredfold** now in this time, houses, and brethren, and sisters, and mothers, and children, and lands, with persecutions; and in the world to come eternal life.'*

(Mark 10:30)

*'And other fell on good ground, and sprang up, and bare fruit an **hundredfold**. And when he had said these things, he cried, He that hath ears to hear, let him hear.'*   (Luke 8:8)

Let us look firstly at the above context in Genesis. If you go to Genesis 26:1 you will see that *'there was a famine in the land'*. Then God spoke to Isaac and gave him strict instructions about where he was to go. He was told not to go to Egypt but to *'dwell in the land which I shall tell thee of'*. It is so important to be in the will of God in the place that God wants us to be otherwise we will not prosper. The Lord then makes a promise to him:

> *'Sojourn in this land, and I will be with thee, and will bless thee; for unto thee, and unto thy seed, I will give all these countries, and I will perform the oath which I sware unto Abraham thy father; And I will make thy seed to multiply as the stars of heaven, and will give unto thy seed all these countries; and in thy seed shall all the nations of the earth be blessed; Because that Abraham obeyed my voice, and kept my charge, my commandments, my statutes, and my laws.'*
> (Genesis 26:3–5)

Even in a depression when the economy was bad Isaac was promised by the Lord Himself that he would prosper in **every area of life**. Further on in the chapter we see the first mention of the hundredfold harvest on our giving in verse 12 already quoted above. The two verses after go even further!

> *'And the man waxed great, and went forward, and grew until he became very great: For he had possession of flocks, and possession of herds, and great store of servants: and the Philistines envied him.'*
> (Genesis 26:13–14)

As we examine verse 12 it says that **'Isaac sowed in the land'**. Isaac was already established in tithing which had been passed to him by his father Abraham (Genesis 14:20).

We only receive the hundredfold return on the offerings we give over and above the tithe! Tithing opens the windows of heaven so that we can sow seeds and reap a harvest for the sake of the kingdom.

Isaac saw a one hundredfold increase in just one year on his giving in the middle of a famine. Hallelujah! Only God can do this! As the people of God we are promised continual increase whatever is happening in the economy of the world because **the world is not our source**. The Lord Himself is our provider.

Isaac just kept increasing until the heathen began to be jealous of his wealth.

Even with all this going on and Isaac prospering God then visits him and makes him a promise:

> *'And the LORD appeared unto him the same night, and said, I am the God of Abraham thy father: fear not, **for I am with thee, and will bless thee, and multiply thy seed** for my servant Abraham's sake.'*   (Genesis 26:24)

He was already seeing an hundredfold return on all his giving, he had already become 'very great' in the sight of the heathen and God visits him and promises him even more abundance!

And this is only the beginning. Let us look at what Jesus says to us in the Gospels.

> *'And Jesus answered and said, Verily I say unto you, There is no man that hath left house, or brethren, or sisters, or father, or mother, or wife, or children, or lands, for my sake, and the Gospel's, But he shall receive an hundredfold now in this time, houses, and brethren, and sisters, and mothers, and children, and lands, with persecutions; and in the world to come eternal life. But many that are first shall be last; and the last first.'*   (Mark 10:29–31)

The last verse here speaks of patience: prosperity comes to patient people who persevere. You cannot escape this verse. Jesus Himself promises us a hundredfold of all things in this life – but do not forget the persecution!

> *'Yea, and all that will live godly in Christ Jesus shall suffer persecution.'*   (2 Timothy 3:12)

The Jews are still persecuted because of their wealth and their covenant was fulfilled nearly two thousand years ago. We are now under the New Covenant which is a more powerful covenant and deals with the whole man, not just the spiritual part of things.

> *'But now hath he obtained a more excellent ministry, **by how much also he is the mediator of a better covenant, which was established upon better promises**. For if that*

first covenant had been faultless, then should no place have been sought for the second. For finding fault with them, he saith, Behold, the days come, saith the Lord, when I will make a new covenant with the house of Israel and with the house of Judah.'   (Hebrews 8:6–8)

Better promises therefore must include all the blessings of the Old and more.

'That the blessing of Abraham might come on the Gentiles through Jesus Christ; *that we might receive the promise of the Spirit through* **faith.'**   (Galatians 3:14)

This verse helped me greatly in understanding prosperity. Abraham was the richest man around in his day and we are promised his blessing!

'And Abraham was old, and well stricken in age: and **the LORD** *had blessed Abraham in all things.'*

(Genesis 24:1)

How much more should we be blessed in all things so that we can fulfil the great commission and preach the Gospel all over the world?

How do we tap into this blessing?

The only scriptural way is by tithing and offering and seeking to give and not to get. As you seek first His kingdom and are rich towards His house you will find that provision, increase and prosperity will come to you in stages. Also we need to maintain a good confession of faith as we have already said. Every time I give my offerings into my church I confess with my mouth an hundredfold return in this life. I also sow specific seeds which we will talk about later.

Incidentally, an hundredfold does not mean an hundred percent as the Strong's definition shows clearly:

'hekatontaplasion . . . : **a hundred times'**

This is much better than any building society rate or stock market promise. They are dealing in small percentages, God is promising us **an hundred times**.

Chapter 9

The Sevenfold Return

We have an enemy and he knows the Scriptures. He understands the principles of God's Word and delights in preventing us from experiencing His best. His name is Satan, or the devil. One of his many titles in the Bible is 'the thief', as Jesus tells us,

> 'The thief cometh not, but for to steal, and to kill, and to destroy: I am come that they might have life, and that they might have it more abundantly.'　　　(John 10:10)

Have you ever felt that the devil has stolen from you? Health, mental alertness, possessions, relationships etc? **He is only doing his job**! If we are in ignorance to the Word of God then the devil will go on stealing again and again until one day we wake up and **put a stop to it**!

In the area of finances we have to walk closely to what God says to prevent Satan from stealing from us. Every time you borrow money you give him a chance to steal from you, every time you do not tithe he gets another bite into your hard-earned finances, rebellion to the Word of God gives Satan another chance. Worry is another inroad for the enemy to rob you. I am glad that the Lord has given us a way back at the devil financially and in every way, to stop him stealing from us ever again. Take a look at this verse of Scripture.

> 'Men do not despise a thief, if he steal to satisfy his soul when he is hungry; But **if he be found, he shall**

> ***restore sevenfold****; he shall give all the substance of his
> house.'*   (Proverbs 6:30–31)

As soon as I found this out I began to command Satan to
bring back everything he had stolen from me sevenfold. The
most amazing thing happened. Up until this time we would
have money taken from us in some form or another. As
soon as we enforced this sevenfold principle on our
finances, not only have we been increasing but **the stealing
has stopped completely**! The devil knows that I will simply
receive seven times back what he takes from me so he does
not bother any more as a general rule. Having said this, he
did do it once this year (1997) and I asked the Lord about it
and God said to me that the devil was so angry that he just
wanted to get at me. However, it backfired into his face and
I am much more blessed because he dared to attack my
finances.

Therefore, as a believer I have the windows of heaven
open since we tithe 52 weeks of the year, I have 100 times
back in this life what I sow as offerings and the devil is
bringing back seven times of all that he stole from me.
Praise God!

Another Scripture that talks about the enemy devouring
finances is in the same passage as tithing:

> *'Bring ye all the tithes into the storehouse, that there may be
> meat in mine house, and prove me now herewith, saith the
> Lord of hosts, if I will not open you the windows of heaven,
> and pour you out a blessing, that there shall not be room
> enough to receive it. And **I will rebuke the devourer for
> your sakes**, and he shall not destroy the fruits of your
> ground; neither shall your vine cast her fruit before the time
> in the field, saith the Lord of hosts. And all nations shall
> call you blessed: for ye shall be a delightsome land, saith the
> Lord of hosts.'*   (Malachi 3:10–12)

Thus when we tithe God rebukes the devourer for our
sakes. Under the New Covenant I strongly believe that **we**
now have the authority to rebuke the devil over our
finances – once we have applied all of what the Word of
God says (particularly if we can sense he is trying to rob us).

As we walk closely to the Lord we can become sensitive to what is happening in the spirit realm and so it is financially. However, you do not have to keep rebuking the devil all the time but only when you can sense his attacks.

> *'Behold, I give unto you power to tread on serpents and scorpions, and over all the power of the enemy: and nothing shall by any means hurt you.'* (Luke 10:19)

> *'Submit yourselves therefore to God. Resist the devil, and he will flee from you.'* (James 4:7)

We have all used these verses in the context of spiritual warfare in the spiritual realm, but what about every other realm? If the enemy has been stealing from you financially or he has done so in the past, then you can get it all back **sevenfold**! I suggest that you write down all the amounts and then tell that rat that he has to restore back to you seven times what he has stolen and then watch what happens. Remember that the devil is under our feet (that is, we have authority over him), so he has no option but to bring it all back. Also he will stop stealing from you! This usually comes as a very pleasant surprise to most believers and sets them on a course of getting back what the devil has taken. Begin today!

Chapter 10

Naming Your Seed

There is a law in the kingdom of God which the Lord Himself established at the beginning of time:

> *'And God said, Let the earth bring forth grass, the herb yielding seed, and **the fruit tree yielding fruit after his kind, whose seed is in itself**, upon the earth: and it was so.'* (Genesis 1:11)

Everything reproduces after its own kind. Once a seed goes into the ground from an apple it can never produce anything but another apple tree. It would be on the front page of all the daily newspapers if oranges grew instead! We all know the natural law of reproduction. So it is in the financial realm. Money is called a seed which we plant into our local church and it produces a harvest.

> *'But this I say, He which soweth sparingly shall reap also sparingly; and he which soweth bountifully shall reap also bountifully. Every man according as he purposeth in his heart, so let him give; not grudgingly, or of necessity: for God loveth a cheerful giver.'* (2 Corinthians 9:6–7)

> *'Now **he that ministereth seed to the sower both minister bread for your food, and multiply your seed sown, and increase the fruits of your righteousness.'*** (2 Corinthians 9:10)

This whole chapter is talking about money from the start.

The Bible also tells us to be specific in our prayers and so when we need finance for personal needs or the work of

God we should pray in faith and then sow a specific seed for that project. If I need £1000 I sow £10 and believe for a one hundredfold return which brings in the money. My wife and I do this all the time and we maintain a debt-free and increasingly prosperous life-style and ministry.

Ruth and I needed a three-piece suite recently since the one we had was nearly thirty years old. We both wanted a leather one which would last a long time. We prayed in faith and also sowed and named our seed. When we moved into our new house recently we decided to throw our old three-piece away. This left us with nothing but an empty space and meant that we were really standing! While I was in Australia my wife told me that someone had offered to pay for the suite of our choice. We chose it and it arrived, paid for, just two weeks before I wrote this chapter. Also when we moved into our home we had no dining table. However, someone had been told by the Lord that we would be moving into our new house at the end of March 1997 and that she should give us her dining table and chairs. We had prayed and sown our seed for a dining table a while ago and the day we moved into our house we were given a superb table to seat eight people. God is so faithful.

Shortly after we moved into our house I was due to go to Australia. We had spent so much extra money moving house that we did not have the money to pay for the airline ticket, which was about £1400. I had ordered the ticket because I knew that God wanted me to go. Two weeks before I was due to leave the country the Holy Spirit reminded me that I had not sown a seed for the money and so I quickly put £15 into the offering at church and named my seed for one thousand five hundred pounds to cover everything. **Within a few days I had the money in full**! Someone gave me an anonymous gift of £1000 and then the rest came in smaller amounts. Praise God!

Ruth and I have been sowing seeds and standing in faith for many large projects such as cars, a house, successive new church buildings, book publications and even a jet! We have sown realistic seeds for all of these things and continue to stand in faith for the manifestation. God speaks to me about things in the financial realm just the same way as He speaks to me about things in the spiritual realm.

One day I was getting into strife about our car because I wanted a new one that very day. I decided to pray until God spoke to me about the car. Ruth went to bed that night while I stayed up to pray through the issue. I began by praying in tongues for about an hour and kept bringing the situation to the Lord. God started to speak to me about His work, and then He gave me a list of things that He wanted me to do for Him. But He made no mention of anything to do with a car. I kept asking about my car and He kept giving me instructions like this: 'Once you have done **this**, then I want you to do **that** and then start this!' I wrote it all down and slowly began to realise where I had been going wrong. I was not 'seeking first the kingdom of God' – instead I was seeking first my car. So what was happening was, as I sought God about a car, He would tell me about His work. This went on for four hours!

By 2 o'clock in the morning I was still seeking God about it and by this time I had filled a whole page of A4 paper with instructions from Him for ministry. Then at 2:30 am, when I thought that He would never speak to me about my need, He gave me a vision of what would eventually happen regarding our car. That was about four years ago and I am still standing in faith for it. However, my present car runs very well and I am now patiently expecting to see our new car manifest in **His** time, not mine. I repented of striving and continued to put His work first. God has a timing for things which we cannot violate.

Listening to His voice

For a while we were believing God for some recording equipment in church to be able to produce cassette tapes. We had no money in the church except for about £40. We wanted a high-speed, double-sided audio cassette copier, which would cost £2700 alone, not counting the other equipment we would need with it. In all, we needed about £4000 to complete the job. The Lord spoke to me and told me to go ahead and buy the equipment! I asked, 'What with?' and made one announcement in church that we were going to buy this necessary equipment in the next four weeks and if anybody wanted to give then that would be fine. I only made one announcement. (We often involve our people in buying for His work, but never our own needs.)

Within two days I was promised £2000! Then someone else gave the church £1700 and the Lord provided the rest in other ways. It pays to listen and obey His voice in finances. We started our church from nothing just under six years ago and already we have everything we need as far as equipment is concerned. Computers, PA system, two overhead projectors, chairs, desks, filing cabinets, two photocopiers, fax machine etc. It is all paid for. We also have a building right in the centre of the city which is a miracle in itself.

Life-Changing Ministries had been going for just two years when we decided to start a building fund for a building of our own. We raised about £2000. Immediately, the Lord spoke to me and told me to sow a specific seed into another building project and to name our seed for a building. We sowed £700 into a building project which was already in progress. Within twelve months of doing this, we were offered our present building which was a second floor office block with 22 offices. I tried to visualise it as a church and struggled to believe that it would be suitable. But it could not have been more perfect for our work! God knew what He wanted for His ministry.

Then came the negotiations with the owners as to how much rent we would pay. The seed was in the ground and doing its work. They asked me how much we could afford for the whole of the top floor and I offered a ridiculously paltry £105 pound per week (although even this was a step of faith because we did not have that much anyway!) The normal lease should have been about £600 per week yet I was offering just £105. I waited for their response and they wholeheartedly agreed to a three-year lease. **Hallelujah**! We had sown a seed one year previously and now we had seen a harvest.

When we moved in the Lord spoke to me and said that

this was just the start from that one seed. Remember when Jesus said this:

> *'For the earth bringeth forth fruit of herself; first the blade, then the ear, after that the full corn in the ear.'*

(Mark 4:28)

God said to me that this building was simply the **blade**. We have yet to see the ear and then the full corn in the ear! Praise God!

You must be specific in sowing and naming your seeds if you want to see the miracles start pouring out to the glory of God. This is the key to staying free of all debt. As soon as you can see that you will need something in the near or distant future, simply pray for it and sow a specific seed into your church and name the seed towards that project. I usually put the name of the seed on my cheque stub. Ruth and I do this in the home with everything. Washing machines, cookers, beds etc. Then when the time comes to buy these items we can pay in cash. This keeps us ahead and never behind.

One day we were believing for a stereo system since our old one had bitten the dust. Unfortunately, we had not sown a seed and so we had to go without for a season. One day I became desperate to be able to listen to worship tapes etc., and I was determining to go and buy a cheap radio cassette player to keep us going. The Spirit of God had already read my mind and spoke to me to wait a bit longer until after Christmas. I obeyed and someone came up to me and gave a huge personal gift which was the right amount, after giving the tithe, to buy an excellent stereo system. Praise God! We believe for the best of everything since God always gives the best to us. He gave us Jesus who is the best!

I suggest that you make two lists today: firstly, a list of all the things that you need to do the Lord's work; and secondly, a personal list of things you would like for yourself. Then sow and name your seeds. Don't forget that **you water your seeds by the confession of your mouth**. If you asked me today if I have my own jet I would say, 'Yes!' I am calling those things which be not as though they were.

God told me to believe for one and so I have taken it seriously.

This happened with my last car. I was believing God and standing in faith for it, and when someone would ask me if I had my car yet, I would reply 'Yes', by faith. One day I said this to a certain Christian friend who mocked me about it – she thought I was being foolish. This was because she did not understand the things of faith. But within a few weeks someone had bought me a Volvo 244DL with only 54,000 miles on the clock! When I next saw that friend she said she felt rebuked by the Lord for her attitude towards my statement of faith. Now she too has this kind of faith.

I also believe I already have my own house paid for and confess it regularly. It works in any area of life when we are seeking first His kingdom. **Prosperity belongs to us**!

Chapter 11

Prosperity Is Relative

What do I mean by this? Well it is quite simple. What is prosperity to one person may not be to someone else. If you went to some countries of the world where they had no food or basic needs and you offered to buy them, for example, a car, this would not be prosperity to them particularly if they could not put fuel into it. Prosperity to them would be food in the short term and the ability to provide for themselves in the long term.

Also, if you compare two people from differing backgrounds – one from a wealthy situation and the other from a poor family – their ideas of prosperity would be very different. That is why we must never judge others when it comes to someone's standard of living. God promises to increase us all **relative to our present circumstances**. Prosperity almost always comes in stages. One step at a time.

Another aspect of relative prosperity is when we compare any one man's wealth with that of **God Himself**! Your ability to produce wealth will never impress **Him**. He is extremely rich. Anyone who can afford to have transparent gold streets and pearls for gates is way out of any earthly league!

> *'And I John saw the holy city, new Jerusalem, coming down from God out of heaven, prepared as a bride adorned for her husband.'* (Revelation 21:2)

> *'And the building of the wall of it was of jasper: and the city was pure gold, like unto clear glass. And the foundations of*

the wall of the city were garnished with all manner of precious stones. The first foundation was jasper; the second, sapphire; the third, a chalcedony; the fourth, an emerald; The fifth, sardonyx; the sixth, sardius; the seventh, chryso-lyte; the eighth, beryl; the ninth, a topaz; the tenth, a chrysoprasus; the eleventh, a jacinth; the twelfth, an amethyst. And the twelve gates were twelve pearls: every several gate was of one pearl: and the street of the city was pure gold, as it were transparent glass.'

(Revelation 21:18–21)

No amount of prosperity on Earth could match this kind of wealth! Let us face real facts here. God is extremely wealthy and prosperous in every way. He is the source of all real wealth.

Prosperity is also an opportunity for evangelism. People of the world are striving all the time to get more of this world's goods. When the Lord blesses His people with something, it creates a God-given opportunity to tell people how we got it, and also to share about the love and grace of God with them. I remember when I received the new car that we had been believing God for. It enabled me to tell many people that my Father in heaven had provided it, and this was used many times to attract people's attention to the Gospel.

On the other hand, if we are always having crisis after crisis financially, what do you think the world is going to think? They are not going to want anything to do with Christianity! You are a witness for the whole man, body, soul and spirit. As people see that we are prospering in our family, for instance, they will eventually take notice of it and see for themselves how God looks after His children.

Chapter 12

Prosperity for the Whole Man

I have looked up a few of the words used for 'prosperity' in the Old Testament and it is most enlightening!

'Shalowm': safe (figuratively) i.e. well, happy, friendly; also (abstractly) welfare, i.e. health, prosperity, peace, (good) health, to be at peace, to prosper. Rest, safety, welfare, for all to be well.

'Shalvah': security, abundance, peace, prosperity, quietness.

'Towb': good (as an adjective) in the widest sense; used likewise as a noun, both in the masculine and the feminine, the singular and the plural (good, a good or good thing, a good man or woman; the good, goods or good things, good men or women), also as an adverb (well): beautiful, best, better, bountiful, cheerful, at ease, fair, (to be in) favour, fine, glad, good, goodly, goodness, graciously, joyful, kindly, kindness, liketh (best), loving, merry, pleasant, pleasure, precious, prosperity, sweet, wealth, welfare, to be well-favoured.

Just these three definitions cover such a broad cross-section of human existence. Praise God for His wonderful care over us in all aspects of life! God is interested in every part of our lives however small or insignificant it may seem. He is such a big God and yet He cares for all the small things as well as the big things. I am glad that He is able to meet with us all at our level with an understanding that no human can comprehend. He is a Father who delights to bless His children in so many ways. I have been amazed at how the Lord takes care of all the little things in life that we may not even think about. When I travel around the world and go to various places He has often surprised me in the little ways that He provides for me. There have been many times when I have simply thought about something that I would like from a particular country and it has been given to me without my even having to pray about it!

> *'And it shall come to pass, that before they call, I will answer; and while they are yet speaking, I will hear.'*
>
> (Isaiah 65:24)

The closer we are to the Lord in fellowship the more we will experience the reality of this wonderful Scripture.

The wealth of the wicked

> *'I have seen the wicked in great power, and spreading himself like a green bay tree. Yet he passed away, and, lo, he was not: yea, I sought him, but he could not be found.'*
>
> (Psalm 37:35–36)

> *'Behold, these are the ungodly, who prosper in the world; they increase in riches.'* (Psalm 73:12)

There are times in life when it appears that the people of the world who are living for themselves, living in sin and caring not for the things of God seem to increase in wealth. It appears with some of them that everything that they do just bears fruit. The Bible warns us that we should not be jealous of them but trust God and be patient. I am going to show you something that is very interesting that will encourage you regarding the wealth of the wicked.

> *'A good man leaveth an inheritance to his children's children: and **the wealth of the sinner is laid up for the just.'*** (Proverbs 13:22)

Therefore, you need to rejoice when the wicked prosper because one day it will all come to us.

> *'For God giveth to a man that is good in his sight wisdom, and knowledge, and joy: but to the sinner he giveth travail, to gather and to heap up, **that he may give to him that is good before God**. This also is vanity and vexation of spirit.'*
> (Ecclesiastes 2:26)

So keep your eyes on the Lord and wait patiently for the financial transfer from the wicked to the just!

The next two generations

The above verse (Proverbs 13:22) gives very strong reassurance indeed regarding prosperity. It says that a good man should leave an inheritance for his children's children. That is real wealth in anyone's language. Not only does God want us to provide for our own and support the work of the Lord but also to bless the next two generations! Imagine if you had 30 grandchildren! No wonder the Bible says that His ways are higher than our ways! (Isaiah 55:8, 9).

> *'Now unto him that is able to do exceeding abundantly above all that we ask or think, according to the power that worketh in us.'*
> (Ephesians 3:20)

I pray that more and more of the people of God will get onto His wavelength in this and every other area of existence to enable the church of Jesus Christ to reach more souls and make us more effective in all ways to glorify God.

Prosperity destroys a fool!

Some people are frightened of prosperity because of what it might do to them. Let us look at the Word of God:

> *'For the turning away of the simple shall slay them, and **the prosperity of fools shall destroy them**.'* (Proverbs 1:32)

This verse is clear enough regarding prosperity. Only fools are destroyed by it! Thus if someone goes astray through the wealth of this world then it only goes to prove that they were fools. Prosperity will not ruin the person who keeps giving to God as he prospers and stays single-minded on the things of God. We should not seek after material things anyway. Concentrate on the Kingdom and let the Lord look after everything else. Once you have prayed in faith for the things of this life then that is the end of the matter. I spend most of my time praying for others and only a very small percentage of my prayer life is spent on me. I would say about two percent of my prayers are for me and my situation. The rest is spent on devotion, worship, praise, intercession, seeking His face, praying for revival etc.

Having a lot of money should not ruin you at all. Rather you should seek for ways to distribute it into the work of the Lord where He leads you. There is always someone in the Kingdom who you can bless with this world's goods or direct financial support. I am constantly looking for someone to bless in our church, since I know what it is like to have nothing and this gives me a much greater awareness of others' needs. If you have plenty of surplus money, why not go and see your Pastor or Minister? I am sure that he knows plenty of ways to bless others! Or why not bless him?

Chapter 13

The Root and Fatness of the Olive Tree

When I first read through the eleventh chapter of Romans as a young Christian I found it very hard to understand. However like many other parts of Scripture I persevered until some light appeared. I think that receiving revelation of God's Word is an ongoing process – the more we seek God and read His word, the more understanding we receive.

> *'And if some of the branches be broken off, and thou, being a wild olive tree, wert grafted in among them, and with them partakest of the root and fatness of the olive tree.'*
>
> (Romans 11:17)

You will understand the above verse much more if I give you a clue. The Jews are referred to as 'the olive tree' whereas the Gentiles are referred to as a 'wild olive tree'.

While I was reading through this chapter the other day I noticed something quite startling regarding prosperity. Look at these verses!

> *'I say then, Have they stumbled that they should fall? God forbid: **but rather through their fall salvation is come unto the Gentiles, for to provoke them to jealousy**. Now if the fall of them be the riches of the world, and **the diminishing of them the riches of the Gentiles**; how much more their fulness?'* (Romans 11:11–12)

These two verses tell us clearly that there has been a transfer of riches from the Jews to the Gentiles! This would be a good way to make anyone in the world jealous! If only the Church of Jesus Christ could catch this revelation to enable us to reach all the ends of the Earth with the precious Gospel. God has already made us rich both spiritually **and financially**. The devil has done a good job by telling us that being poor is being humble! In fact the Bible says that poverty is a **curse**!

> *'The curse of the* LORD *is in the house of the wicked: but he blesseth the habitation of the just.'* (Proverbs 3:33)

Never exalt poverty and lack or else it will follow you all the days of your life. Instead believe the Word of God that we are blessed by Him in all things. Faith is released by the confession of our mouth in agreement with the Word of God, but if you ignore what God says then it will not benefit you.

In the old days a man set sail from England to New York on a big ship. He had bought his ticket and took some food with him for the journey. Every time the meals were served on board ship the other passengers would notice this man getting out his sandwiches etc. This went on all through the long voyage which took about two weeks. Right at the end of the journey one of the stewards came up to him and asked him why he did not come to dine at all the sumptuous meals. The man said that he had only bought a ticket for the journey. The steward then told him that **all the meals were included**! He had gone all the way across the Atlantic in total ignorance, not knowing that all the time he could have eaten well.

So it is with many believers. They have their 'ticket' of salvation but are not enjoying the rest of their inheritance. Healing, peace of mind, deliverance, victory and prosperity.

Paul also tells us in Romans 11 that since the majority of the Jews rejected Jesus as their Messiah, for whom they are still waiting today, their riches have been passed on to us. The only way to receive these riches is by faith, like anything else in the Word. You have to agree with it and confess it as yours by right.

Whichever way you look at prosperity in the Bible, it is a wholly consistent principle. **It is the Lord's absolute will to**

bless and prosper you as a child of God, so that you in turn can be a blessing to others. Do not be like the man on board ship going through your Christian life and missing out on all of God's best.

> *'Beloved, I wish above all things that thou mayest prosper and be in health, even as thy soul prospereth.'*   (3 John 2)

If our soul is prospering then we have a God-given right to health and wealth.

> *'The blessing of the* Lord, *it maketh rich, and he addeth no sorrow with it.'*   (Proverbs 10:22)

This is the difference between worldly riches and riches from the Lord. God can make us rich without the sorrow. Take a look at the Jews today. They are still prospering by applying parts of the Old Covenant. We have the **whole** of God's word, so how much more should we be blessed to demonstrate the goodness of God towards His children? Read through Romans 11 and see for yourself.

Chapter 14

Wisom From the Proverbs

The Book of Proverbs has much to say about money and possessions and so we will now take a tour through it to glean some thoughts to ponder.

*'My son, walk not thou in the way with them; refrain thy foot from their path: For their feet run to evil, and make haste to shed blood. Surely in vain the net is spread in the sight of any bird. And they lay wait for their own blood; they lurk privily for their own lives. **So are the ways of every one that is greedy of gain**; which taketh away the life of the owners thereof.'* (Proverbs 1:15–19)

*'For the turning away of the simple shall slay them, and **the prosperity of fools shall destroy them**.'*
(Proverbs 1:32)

'Happy is the man that findeth wisdom, and the man that getteth understanding. For the merchandise of it is better than the merchandise of silver, and the gain thereof than fine gold. She is more precious than rubies: and all the things thou canst desire are not to be compared unto her. Length of days is in her right hand; and in her left hand riches and honour. Her ways are ways of pleasantness, and all her paths are peace.' (Proverbs 3:13–17)

'Yet a little sleep, a little slumber, a little folding of the hands to sleep: So shall thy poverty come as one that travelleth, and thy want as an armed man.'
(Proverbs 6:10–11)

'For by means of a whorish woman a man is brought to a piece of bread: and the adulteress will hunt for the precious life.'   (Proverbs 6:26)

'Riches and honour are with me; yea, durable riches and righteousness. My fruit is better than gold, yea, than fine gold; and my revenue than choice silver. I lead in the way of righteousness, in the midst of the paths of judgment: **That I may cause those that love me to inherit substance; and I will fill their treasures.**'   (Proverbs 8:18–21)

'The Lord *will not suffer the soul of the righteous to famish: but he casteth away the substance of the wicked.* **He becometh poor that dealeth with a slack hand: but the hand of the diligent maketh rich.**'   (Proverbs 10:3–4)

'The rich man's wealth is his strong city: the destruction of the poor is their poverty.'   (Proverbs 10:15)

'Riches profit not in the day of wrath: but righteousness delivereth from death.'   (Proverbs 11:4)

'A gracious woman retaineth honour: and strong men retain riches.'   (Proverbs 11:16)

'There is that scattereth, and yet increaseth; and there is that withholdeth more than is meet, but it tendeth to poverty.'   (Proverbs 11:24)

'The liberal soul shall be made fat: and he that watereth shall be watered also himself.'   (Proverbs 11:25)

'He that trusteth in his riches shall fall: but the righteous shall flourish as a branch.'   (Proverbs 11:28)

'Behold, **the righteous shall be recompensed in the earth***: much more the wicked and the sinner.'*

(Proverbs 11:31)

'The soul of the sluggard desireth, and hath nothing: but the soul of the diligent shall be made fat.'   (Proverbs 13:4)

'There is that maketh himself rich, yet hath nothing: there is that maketh himself poor, yet hath great riches.'

(Proverbs 13:7)

'Wealth gotten by vanity shall be diminished: but he that gathereth by labour shall increase.'
(Proverbs 13:11)

'Poverty and shame shall be to him that refuseth instruction: but he that regardeth reproof shall be honoured.' (Proverbs 13:18)

'A good man leaveth an inheritance to his children's children: and the wealth of the sinner is laid up for the just.'
(Proverbs 13:22)

'The righteous eateth to the satisfying of his soul: but the belly of the wicked shall want.' (Proverbs 13:25)

'The house of the wicked shall be overthrown: but **the tabernacle of the upright shall flourish.'**
(Proverbs 14:11)

'The poor is hated even of his own neighbour: but the rich hath many friends.' (Proverbs 14:20)

'In all labour there is profit: but the talk of the lips tendeth only to penury.' (Proverbs 14:23)

'The crown of the wise is their riches: but the foolishness of fools is folly.' (Proverbs 14:24)

'He that oppresseth the poor reproacheth his Maker: but he that honoureth him hath mercy on the poor.'
(Proverbs 14:31)

'In the house of the righteous is much treasure: but in the revenues of the wicked is trouble.' (Proverbs 15:6)

'Better is little with the fear of the LORD than great treasure and trouble therewith. *Better is a dinner of herbs where love is, than a stalled ox and hatred therewith.'*
(Proverbs 15:16–17)

'The LORD will destroy the house of the proud: but **he will establish the border of the widow.'** (Proverbs 15:25)

'He that is greedy of gain troubleth his own house; *but he that hateth gifts shall live.'* (Proverbs 15:27)

'Better is a little with righteousness than great revenues without right.'   (Proverbs 16:8)

'How much better is it to get wisdom than gold! and to get understanding rather to be chosen than silver!'
                                                    (Proverbs 16:16)

'Better it is to be of an humble spirit with the lowly, than to divide the spoil with the proud.'   (Proverbs 16:19)

'Whoso mocketh the poor reproacheth his Maker: and he that is glad at calamities shall not be unpunished.'
                                                    (Proverbs 17:5)

'Better is the poor that walketh in his integrity, than he that is perverse in his lips, and is a fool.'*   (Proverbs 19:1)

'Wealth maketh many friends; but the poor is separated from his neighbour.'   (Proverbs 19:4)

'House and riches are the inheritance of fathers: and a prudent wife is from the Lᴏʀᴅ.'*   (Proverbs 19:14)

*'Slothfulness casteth into a deep sleep; and **an idle soul shall suffer hunger**.'*   (Proverbs 19:15)

'He that hath pity upon the poor lendeth unto the Lᴏʀᴅ; and that which he hath given will he pay him again.'   (Proverbs 19:17)

'The sluggard will not plow by reason of the cold; therefore shall he beg in harvest, and have nothing.' (Proverbs 20:4)

*'The just man walketh in his integrity: **his children are blessed after him**.'*   (Proverbs 20:7)

'Love not sleep, lest thou come to poverty; open thine eyes, and thou shalt be satisfied with bread.'*
                                                    (Proverbs 20:13)

'An inheritance may be gotten hastily at the beginning; but the end thereof shall not be blessed.'   (Proverbs 20:21)

'The thoughts of the diligent tend only to plenteousness; but of every one that is hasty only to want.'
                                                    (Proverbs 21:5)

'The getting of treasures by a lying tongue is a vanity tossed to and fro of them that seek death.' (Proverbs 21:6)

'Whoso stoppeth his ears at the cry of the poor, he also shall cry himself, but shall not be heard.'

(Proverbs 21:13)

'He that loveth pleasure shall be a poor man: he that loveth wine and oil shall not be rich.'

(Proverbs 21:17)

'There is treasure to be desired and oil in the dwelling of the wise; but a foolish man spendeth it up.'

(Proverbs 21:20)

'The desire of the slothful killeth him; for his hands refuse to labour. He coveteth greedily all the day long: but the righteous giveth and spareth not.'

(Proverbs 21:25–26)

'A good name is rather to be chosen than great riches, *and loving favour rather than silver and gold.'*

(Proverbs 22:1)

'The rich and poor meet together: the Lord **is the maker of them all.'** (Proverbs 22:2)

'By humility and the fear of the Lord **are riches, and honour, and life.'** (Proverbs 22:4)

'The rich ruleth over the poor, and the borrower is servant to the lender.' (Proverbs 22:7)

'He that hath a bountiful eye shall be blessed; for he giveth of his bread to the poor.' (Proverbs 22:9)

'He that oppresseth the poor to increase his riches, and he that giveth to the rich, shall surely come to want.'

(Proverbs 22:16)

'Rob not the poor, because he is poor: *neither oppress the afflicted in the gate: For the* Lord *will plead their cause, and spoil the soul of those that spoiled them.'*

(Proverbs 22:22–23)

'Seest thou a man diligent in his business? he shall stand before kings; *he shall not stand before mean men.'*
(Proverbs 22:29)

'Labour not to be rich: cease from thine own wisdom.'
(Proverbs 23:4)

'Wilt thou set thine eyes upon that which is not? for riches certainly make themselves wings; they fly away as an eagle toward heaven.'   (Proverbs 23:5)

'For the drunkard and the glutton shall come to poverty: and drowsiness shall clothe a man with rags.'
(Proverbs 23:21)

'Through wisdom is an house builded; and by understanding it is established: And by knowledge shall the chambers be filled with all precious and pleasant riches.'
(Proverbs 24:3–4)

'I went by the field of the slothful, and by the vineyard of the man void of understanding; *And, lo, it was all grown over with thorns, and nettles had covered the face thereof, and the stone wall thereof was broken down. Then I saw, and considered it well: I looked upon it, and received instruction.'*   (Proverbs 24:30–32)

'Yet a little sleep, a little slumber, a little folding of the hands to sleep: So shall thy poverty come *as one that travelleth; and thy want as an armed man.'*
(Proverbs 24:33–34)

'He that by usury and unjust gain increaseth his substance, he shall gather it for him that will pity the poor.'   (Proverbs 28:8)

'He that covereth his sins shall not prosper: *but whoso confesseth and forsaketh them shall have mercy.'*
(Proverbs 28:13)

'The prince that wanteth understanding is also a great oppressor: **but he that hateth covetousness shall prolong his days.'**   (Proverbs 28:16)

'He that tilleth his land shall have plenty of bread: but he that followeth after vain persons shall have poverty enough.'
(Proverbs 28:19)

'A faithful man shall abound with blessings: but he that maketh haste to be rich shall not be innocent.'
(Proverbs 28:20)

*'He that is of a proud heart stirreth up strife: but **he that putteth his trust in the** LORD **shall be made fat.'***
(Proverbs 28:25)

'He that giveth unto the poor shall not lack: but he that hideth his eyes shall have many a curse.'
(Proverbs 28:27)

Much wisdom indeed! This gives us warning about many things that will affect our prosperity. Lazy people will never prosper. Those who ignore the poor will be in want themselves. Drunkenness and gluttony are two major hindrances to prosperity. Meditate on these verses in order to draw your own conclusions, and then examine your life and see if any changes need to be made.

Chapter 15

Job

People have drawn many mistaken conclusions about the character of God from this story, and I would like to address some of these. We will begin at the start of the book:

> *'There was a man in the land of Uz,* **whose name was Job; and that man was perfect and upright, and one that feared God, and eschewed evil.** *And there were born unto him seven sons and three daughters.* **His substance also was seven thousand sheep, and three thousand camels, and five hundred yoke of oxen, and five hundred she asses, and a very great household; so that this man was the greatest of all the men of the east.'**

(Job 1:1–3)

Job was a man of God who hated evil and lived in reverence for the Lord. He was a very rich man and according to the above verse was probably the richest in the world at that time. Please read the whole of chapter one for yourself and then examine the following points.

In verse 5 it is revealed that even though Job was a righteous man he lived in a constant state of worry about his children. He did not even know for sure that his children had sinned and yet he kept making the same sacrifices continually. This shows us that Job was in fear, worry and unbelief. In practice, fear is **faith in the devil**, and it caused the hedge of protection around Job's children to come down, allowing Satan to destroy them. God told Satan that all that Job had was in his power, which meant that Job must have been in fear and worry about other things also even though he was a righteous man. Thus he lost his possessions also.

The Bible tells us that Job kept a right attitude towards God in all this even though his wife wanted him to curse God and die (Job 2:9).

In chapter 3 Job realises what happened and admits that it was all his fault.

> *'For the thing which I greatly feared is come upon me, and that which I was afraid of is come unto me.'*
>
> (Job 3:25)

Therefore it was not **God** that robbed Job of his family or wealth but **Satan, because of fear on Job's part**. We often do not realise what a major part our thinking has to play in the circumstances of our life!

The New Testament reveals a characteristic about Job which is a credit to him.

> *'Behold, we count them happy which endure. Ye have heard of the patience of Job, and have seen the end of the Lord; that the Lord is very pitiful, and of tender mercy.'*
>
> (James 5:11)

Job went through a very traumatic time in his life, although Bible scholars tell me it only lasted for about nine months to a year at the most. (I used to think that the 42 chapters of this book depicted many years in the life of Job because of the length of it!)

Look at the end of the book:

> *'And the LORD turned the captivity of Job, when he prayed for his friends: **also the LORD gave Job twice as much as he had before.'*** (Job 42:10)

> *'So the LORD blessed the latter end of Job more than his beginning: for he had fourteen thousand sheep, and six thousand camels, and a thousand yoke of oxen, and a thousand she asses.'* (Job 42:12)

You will also notice that the wife of Job is never mentioned again after her dreadful attitude was revealed in chapter 2.

Thus we can see that Job allowed Satan into his life through fear and worry, and that this caused devastating effects on both his family and material possessions. However, his heart was right with the Lord and once he recognised and repented of the fear which had caused the disasters in his life, the Lord blessed him twice as much as before. Which meant that he was now extremely rich!

Thus we can learn much from this story regarding prosperity as well as many other aspects of life. Firstly, be pure and upright with God in all things. Hate evil and try to please God in everything you do. Also make sure that you are in faith in every area of life and do not allow fear, worry or anxiety to take hold of you. We all have to fight these forces from time to time but God tells us that we can have the victory **all** the time. Take a look at the following Scriptures:

> *'Be careful for nothing; but in every thing by prayer and supplication with thanksgiving let your requests be made known unto God.'* (Philippians 4:6)

The word *'careful'* here means the following:

> *'Merimnao'*: to be anxious about, to have care, to be careful or take thought.

Therefore we are told not to worry or be anxious, but to pray about everything in life and give the burden to God and let Him take care of it.

> *'Casting all your care upon him; for he careth for you.'*
> (1 Peter 5:7)

> *'There is no fear in love; but perfect love casteth out fear: because fear hath torment. He that feareth is not made perfect in love.'* (1 John 4:18)

These verses are abundantly clear. We are meant to lead a worry-free life by trusting God in all things. That is why we should spend much quality time in the Word of God and to fill our hearts with the life-changing eternal Word of God. Faith, confidence and trust develop as we meditate on His Word. His Word has the power to transform us into bold, fearless and victorious children of God who will make a lasting impact on our world.

Job learnt a very painful lesson which we should all learn from too so that we do not fall into the same trap. However, I am glad that our wonderful Father in heaven is so patient and full of compassion towards us even when we do sin and fall short of His standards. The accounts in the Bible about other peoples' mistakes are there to help us not to make those same mistakes again. Then we can go on living a life of increase as we are faithful at each step and remain humble enough to give God all the Praise and all the Glory for His goodness towards us. I will leave this chapter with a sobering Scripture for us all.

*'But he that knew not, and did commit things worthy of stripes, shall be beaten with few stripes. **For unto whomsoever much is given, of him shall be much required: and to whom men have committed much, of him they will ask the more.**'* (Luke 12:48)

Chapter 16

The Heart of Solomon

'In that night did God appear unto Solomon, and said unto him, Ask what I shall give thee. And Solomon said unto God, Thou hast showed great mercy unto David my father, and hast made me to reign in his stead. Now, O LORD God, let thy promise unto David my father be established: for thou hast made me king over a people like the dust of the earth in multitude. Give me now wisdom and knowledge, that I may go out and come in before this people: for who can judge this thy people, that is so great? **And God said to Solomon, Because this was in thine heart, and thou hast not asked riches, wealth, or honour, nor the life of thine enemies, neither yet hast asked long life; but hast asked wisdom and knowledge for thyself, that thou mayest judge my people, over whom I have made thee king: Wisdom and knowledge is granted unto thee; and I will give thee riches, and wealth, and honour, such as none of the kings have had that have been before thee, neither shall there any after thee have the like.'**

(2 Chronicles 1:7–12)

In his heart Solomon was not seeking the riches of this world but the Kingdom of God. He wanted wisdom to be able to carry out the work **God** had given him to do. This is the reason why the Lord promised him vast riches.

Notice that Solomon was asleep when the Lord spoke to him (1 Kings 3:5–15).

The Lord knows exactly what is in our hearts and we can

never fool Him into thinking otherwise. He knows when we are proud, arrogant, haughty or self-exalting. He knows everything about us. He knows our deepest motives and attitudes and rewards us accordingly.

> *'Blessed is the man that trusteth in the* LORD, *and whose hope the* LORD *is. For he shall be as a tree planted by the waters, and that spreadeth out her roots by the river, and shall not see when heat cometh, but her leaf shall be green; and shall not be careful in the year of drought, neither shall cease from yielding fruit. The heart is deceitful above all things, and desperately wicked: who can know it? I the* LORD *search the heart, I try the reins, even to give every man according to his ways, and according to the fruit of his doings.'*   (Jeremiah 17:7–10)

Consequently we can see that God gives to us according to our ways and our doings.

Solomon became the richest man of his time according to the Word of God and could have been even greater if he had not been led astray by his many wives and concubines. God knew He could trust Solomon with great prosperity because He knew Solomon had a humble heart. I wonder what God would find in our hearts if He were to search right now? Are we single-minded about His work? Do we have a pure attitude towards others who prosper? Or do we judge those who have wealth? Do we ignore the cry of the poor when we can help them?

Honesty, truth and integrity are vital if we are to prosper correctly.

> *'Let them shout for joy, and be glad, that favour my righteous cause: yea, let them say continually, Let the* LORD *be magnified, which hath pleasure in the prosperity of his servant.'*   (Psalm 35:27)

Chapter 17

Honouring a Servant of the Lord

I have been a pastor for many years and more recently have visited many churches both in the UK and abroad. Therefore I feel qualified to say the following things regarding financial remuneration and the ministry. First of all let us look at the Scriptures with reference to those who are full-time preachers;

> *'Let the elders that rule well be counted worthy of double honour, especially they who labour in the word and doctrine. For the Scripture saith, Thou shalt not muzzle the ox that treadeth out the corn. And, The labourer is worthy of his reward.'* (1 Timothy 5:17–18)

The phrase 'double honour' actually means double stipend. The Strong's Concordance says it derives from a root word meaning 'a value', i.e. money paid, or (concretely and collectively) valuables; by analogy, esteem (especially of the highest degree), or the dignity itself. Honour, precious or price.

Thus a pastor should be treated with the highest esteem and honour in every respect including financially. You have heard the saying 'you always get what you pay for'. This is certainly true in this respect. If you want the best then pay the most! God could always remove a man of God and give you someone else. If you treasure your pastor then look after him in every way possible.

One of the main reasons why Paul gives this instruction I believe is because being in full-time ministry involves so many expenses: transport, telephone, hospitality and foreign missions to name but a few. Unfortunately, many members of a congregation only see their pastor for a few hours each week and so the vast majority of people have little or no idea how hard he actually works. I know many faithful congregations who appreciate their pastor and are very supportive. But others will allow their minister to suffer in silence (since most men of God would not complain to avoid harming the Gospel). If you have a say in your church about this then make every effort to take good care of the ministers and you will reap the benefits!

> *'For it is written in the law of Moses, Thou shalt not muzzle the mouth of the ox that treadeth out the corn. Doth God take care for oxen? Or saith he it altogether for our sakes? For our sakes, no doubt, this is written: that he that ploweth should plow in hope; and that he that thresheth in hope should be partaker of his hope.* **If we have sown unto you spiritual things, is it a great thing if we shall reap your carnal things?** *If others be partakers of this power over you, are not we rather? Nevertheless we have not used this power;* **but suffer all things, lest we should hinder the gospel of Christ.** *Do ye not know that they which minister about holy things live of the things of the temple? and they which wait at the altar are partakers with the altar?* **Even so hath the Lord ordained that they which preach the gospel should live of the gospel.'** (1 Corinthians 9:9–14)

I know that many pastors, including myself, have suffered all things as the above verses say, so that the work of the Gospel goes ahead. Very few people are aware of the tremendous sacrifices that are involved for a pastor and his precious family. Many such men have given up tremendous salaries to obey God in the ministry. I know in my own case that my earning potential in the world is far beyond what I would naturally be able to be paid in the ministry. My wife also could earn a huge salary if she went to work in the world but instead we have chosen to trust our wonderful Father in heaven to provide for us and He does so in many amazing ways. In fact, He has promised that He will bless me in this life beyond any salary I could earn in the world.

Even though it appears to be impossible at the moment, I believe it.

Many ministers are in the same position, having the ability to earn huge salaries in the world but foregoing them out of obedience to the call of the ministry. If it had not been the Lord who has looked after us over the years then we would have died of starvation at least a hundred times over! In all of our time in the ministry Ruth and I have had to pray in faith and believe God for food, clothing, air fares, cars etc. The Lord has always provided for us in awesome ways.

I remember one time when someone bought me a lovely car. The only problem was that we had to insure it! It cost us our whole month's salary at that time and we had to go 33 days without food and petrol. I said to God that we had no money for the entire 33-day period and so He would have to bring it all in. I never told anyone our need. Our children were very young at that time and needed all kinds of special things. The Lord provided throughout that whole period for us with gifts coming in from all over the place.

I have to say that it has never been easy having to trust like this and I have often been tempted to give up and take a well paid job. I am sure that all pastors feel this way regularly. I went for an interview a few years ago to see if God wanted me to take this particular job or to stay a full-time pastor. I said to Him that I would take the job if I was offered it or I would give my whole self to the work of the Lord and trust Him if I did not get it. It was a basic selling job offering £30,000 a year and a new car every year. I went for both interviews and they said that they were very interested in me. It looked like I would get the job since there was no other applicant. I received a letter saying that I had been refused and so I have kept my vow in staying full-time in the ministry and trusting God for much of our income, which we still have to do!

Looking after a travelling ministry

> '*Now ye Philippians know also, that in the beginning of the gospel, when I departed from Macedonia, **no church***

communicated with me as concerning giving and receiving, but ye only.'   (Philippians 4:15)

What a sad thing for Paul to have to write! However, having travelled around the world to different places I have to say that it is only very few churches that know anything about looking after someone who has travelled a long way. Obviously there are some places that you go to and they have nothing financial that they can give because of extreme poverty or devaluation of local currency etc. However, I have visited some very prosperous churches, often spending much money myself to travel there, and been given next to nothing by the people. I am glad that God looks after me! There are some churches that I have been to who are very generous, and they usually make up for those churches who abuse me financially.

What should a church do who has a visiting speaker? The very least thing that should happen is **they should take up an offering every time the speaker ministers**. I am amazed that this rarely happens. A church can then add to those offerings from the church funds if they want to. Give the people a chance to bless the visiting speaker. By doing this you will make sure that the Lord will always provide you with the best ministry. You get what you pay for!

I have been to big churches and also to small churches and some times the smaller churches are far more generous than the big ones. I pray that, for the sake of the Gospel, every church wakes up to this principle of giving financially, both for pastors and to travelling ministers, thereby increasing the quality all round so that everybody benefits!

Chapter 18

Presumption and the Timing of the Lord

'To every thing there is a season, and a time to every purpose under the heaven: A time to be born, and a time to die; a time to plant, and a time to pluck up that which is planted.' (Ecclesiastes 3:1–2)

*'Now I say, That the heir, as long as he is a child, differeth nothing from a servant, though he be lord of all; But is under tutors and governors **until the time appointed of the father**. Even so we, when we were children, were in bondage under the elements of the world: **But when the fulness of the time was come, God sent forth his Son**, made of a woman, made under the law.'* (Galatians 4:1–4)

God always has a time for everything in His kingdom and many sincere believers have found themselves in trouble financially because they **did not want to wait for His perfect timing**!

The Lord may show you a project that He wants you to do for Him but it may take years before it is realised. There are steps that we must take to ensure that we do not go beyond His instructions or fall behind. Sadly, too many have tried to run before they can walk and presumed that God will finance their own ideas. But the Lord will only finance work that **He** has ordained.

*'I am the vine, ye are the branches: He that abideth in me, and I in him, the same bringeth forth much fruit: **for without me ye can do nothing**.'* (John 15:5)

We are simply servants of His instructions. Let me give you an illustration. The Lord had called upon me to write a book called *The Ministry of Jesus Christ*. I worked diligently on it for a long time and finally it was ready for publication. We had no money at that time to even think of publishing another book. We sent the book off to New Wine Press for consideration and a few months later they agreed that they would publish it. Even though they agreed we still did not give them the go-ahead since we did not have any money. The months passed by and still we had no money but I was determined not to act out of presumption. I have made too many mistakes in the past and this has caused me to be extremely careful when it comes to financial outlay.

After eighteen months the money began to come in, until finally we had nearly £5000 to publish our first major international book. For many months it had looked like we would never receive the money, but God is faithful. *The Ministry of Jesus Christ* is now bearing fruit in this country and all over the world. Someone took it to Cambodia where it was translated into Campuchian and is now being used to train pastors in the Phnom Pehn Bible School. It was also used recently at a Tokyo pastors' conference on the ministry gifts. God's timing is perfect!

> '*That ye be not slothful, but followers of them who through faith and patience inherit the promises.* For when God made promise to Abraham, because he could swear by no greater, he sware by himself, Saying, **Surely blessing I will bless thee, and multiplying I will multiply thee.** And so, **after he had patiently endured**, he obtained the promise.'   (Hebrews 6:12–15)

I know a ministry (which will remain nameless) that has had difficulties many times because their philosophy is to keep pushing forward with their own ideas and praying God will finance them. This is not scriptural! This particular ministry is always in debt and has a continual track record of owing people money that it cannot repay. This is not the way to do it. I once challenged its leaders on this subject and they replied, 'How else would we advance?' They also said that they did not know another ministry that was debt-free all the time! **We are! And we shall stay that way!** It appears to be the slow way but it is the sure way.

I like the story of the tortoise and the hare. One day they set out on a race. Immediately the hare raced off and in a very short time was well in the lead. He thought to himself, 'I'll just take a rest under this tree and finish the race later.' He then went to sleep while the tortoise continued to plod along at a slow, steady pace. As the tortoise kept going, he eventually reached the finish line. The hare awoke just in time to see this and frantically tried to catch up, but he was too late. The tortoise won the race.

I have often thought how much I feel like that tortoise in the work of the Lord. It seems so slow sometimes, especially when waiting for finances to come in. But all we have to do is to keep on obeying God's commands and being patient for His timing as to when to go ahead.

A while ago we were renting a Scout hut for our church services, but we were becoming desperate for a building of our own. The ministry was expanding rapidly and we were outgrowing the little hut. Since we had no place to keep our sound equipment etc., members of the congregation were having to bring it every week in their cars. I can hear many of you saying, 'We've been there!' Pioneer work is fun at times but you don't half get stretched.

We were believing for our own building and had done everything that we knew to get one. However, in the centre of a city buildings are very expensive and everything that we looked at was way out of our league. Once again patience paid off because we were offered a building by the Methodist church right in the centre of our city. It has turned out to be such a blessing and the work has prospered so much in the last three years that I am glad that we waited for His perfect timing!

Financial captivities turned

You may be in a financial captivity at the moment and you are doing all that you know to get out of it. You are obeying everything that the Word of God says to do and yet you are still facing problems. If the situation was caused by your own presumption, perhaps by running before you could walk or some other error, then you need to repent of this before the Lord can deliver you. I can assure you that, as a believer in Christ Jesus, God is absolutely committed to rescuing you from your situation and delivering you. However, we must abide by His timing!

> *'When the LORD turned again the captivity of Zion, we were like them that dream. Then was our mouth filled with laughter, and our tongue with singing: then said they among the heathen, The LORD hath done great things for them. The LORD hath done great things for us; whereof we are glad. Turn again our captivity, O LORD, as the streams in the south. They that sow in tears shall reap in joy. He that goeth forth and weepeth, bearing precious seed, shall doubtless come again with rejoicing, bringing his sheaves with him.'* (Psalm 126:1–6)

Most of us have been through a wilderness period at some time or another when it did not look like we would ever come out of it. A financial wilderness is especially trying and affects you emotionally and in every way. We know because we have been there. Ruth and I made some mistakes financially many years ago that put us in a terrible state. We were threatened with no less than **four** County Court judgements which we could not pay. We felt so helpless and alone. I will admit there were times when I wanted to die! It was as if heaven was closed and God didn't care. We knew what the Bible said and tried to believe it and confess it as much as we could. We did everything we knew to do and still nothing happened. It seemed we were being eaten alive by debt and nothing was improving.

Then God spoke to me to start Life-Changing Ministries. As soon as I obeyed His command money started to come in from everywhere to pay off the debt. I was a financial adviser at the time on a commission-only job and I was not selling anything! But after I started LCM, I began to enjoy tremendous success in my job, and became one of the top salesmen in my office in a very short time. The blessing of God had returned to our lives and the debt started to shrink. Finally we paid off everything and have been free of debt ever since.

Seek His face if you are in a similar situation and see if you are harbouring any disobedience or sin that you need to repent of. Has God told you to do something and you have refused Him? Prosperity always comes to obedient Christians.

> *'If ye be willing and obedient, ye shall eat the good of the land: But if ye refuse and rebel, ye shall be devoured with the sword: for the mouth of the L*ORD *hath spoken it.'*   (Isaiah 1:19–20)

Pay careful attention to this aspect of finances regarding presumption and the timing of God and it will save you a lot of heartache. **Then you will stay the head instead of becoming the tail!**

Chapter 19

Big Projects and
the Voice of the Lord

*'And I say also unto thee, That thou art Peter, and upon this rock **I will build my church**; and the gates of hell shall not prevail against it.'*   (Matthew 16:18)

'My sheep hear my voice, and I know them, and they follow me.'   (John 10:27)

Jesus meant this when He said it. He is the master builder of all things and we are simply His servants. He knows the overall plan as well as all the intervening steps regarding how and when every ministry should expand.

I remember reading one person's testimony a few years ago which inspired me greatly. It was about a large building project. He wanted to buy a large old house for a Bible school and also living quarters. It was for sale at £600,000 and this ministry operates a debt-free policy. The leaders took up several offerings and over a period of time they raised £300,000, which was a wonderful achievement. They had been extremely prayerful about this building and had had several confirmations about it from the Lord, so their faith was built up to the point where they were sure that it was God's will. They decided to use the £300,000 they had raised as a deposit since someone else was interested in the building. They then had to pay the balance by a certain date or else they would lose it. But as soon as they had paid the deposit all money stopped coming in. The leader of the organisation then had to go abroad on a speaking engagement and would not be back until the very day that the payment was due!

While he was away an acquaintance came up to him and enquired about the situation. The leader told him that the final balance had to be paid in a few days, but that they still needed £300,000. The acquaintance then said that **he would pay it all for them** – and sure enough, the money went into the ministry's account on the very morning of the day it had to be paid! But the leader said that he had never been anxious about how the money would reach them, even up until the last moment – he knew that God would not let them down.

I have been in similar situations regarding faith ventures where we dare to believe God all the way without borrowing any money. It has always worked and I believe that it always will work – to the glory of God!

I believe that the key is to know His voice by walking closely with Him. At the moment, we are rapidly out-growing our city-centre building and we will shortly need a larger place for our main meetings. However, the Lord has already begun organising this! About four years ago the Lord showed me a piece of land in our city which is huge – 150,000 sq. feet! I felt Him say to me, '*This is your land.*' I did nothing about it and told nobody. The next two years went by and several people spoke prophetically to me and said that that piece of land is ours. All of these people knew nothing about what God had said to me. Even though I had had all this confirmation I still did nothing. One day the Lord spoke clearly to me and said, '*Go and speak over the land what I tell you to say.*'

Let me give a bit of history about this land. Many businesses have made attempts to purchase it for various projects but have all discovered that there is a network of mine shafts beneath it which prevent any building work going ahead.

I went and stood on this land and the Word of the Lord came to me. '*Command the fault to heal.*' I did as I was commanded and then there was silence. I had fulfilled the next step. Within two days a sign appeared saying that a huge building project was about to be started. I was temporarily confused by this since I thought that **we** would end up buying this land. It is so important not to be hasty! I telephoned the building company and found out what was going on. They told me that a business had bought the land and were planning to build six different sized buildings. From the dimensions given to me I was able to work out that these would seat 500, 800, 1000, 1200 and a massive 5000! I slowly realised that the corporations of the world were being used by God to prepare our city for revival! He knows what He is doing but it usually takes us a while to catch up with Him. It must be costing them millions of pounds to build such a complex!

The building company promised that the work would begin in April of 1996. Nothing happened until about a whole year later but as I am writing this book there are all kinds of machines preparing the ground for the foundations. I believe that the Lord will give me the next step when the timing is right. I am a patient man. Five years have come and gone and the foundations are only just being laid now. In the fullness of time!

When you go the way of absolute faith without going into debt, you have nothing to worry about except simply to obey each command from the Father. That is all we are required to do since this is His work and not ours. Without Him we are nothing. We are totally dependent upon Him: we cannot take one step forward without God. My entire life is spent seeking His face in preparation for the next step and I do not attempt to hasten that step in any area of my life. This is how the life of faith works. I never take any step without being sure. It is better to drag your feet a little than to charge ahead before the right time. I used to be the kind of person who would rush in where angels fear to tread but I have learnt the hard way and am more like the tortoise now! However, I am seeing more fruit in the kingdom of God today than I could ever have dreamed about before.

I am glad that the Lord never gives up on us even when we fall flat on our faces. He is there to pick us up and teach us through our foolishness. He is totally committed to us and believes that we will make it and become useful in the kingdom. He has a lot of faith!

Sowing specific seeds

I have already mentioned about sowing £700 as a specific seed for our building project years ago. This is how I have prepared for big projects now for many years. When a farmer wants a crop in a year's time, he plants the necessary seeds for his harvest. It is the same way in finances. My wife and I have sown many seeds for our own house which we are believing will be debt-free and without a mortgage. We have sown seeds for our new cars and named our seeds to produce our cars paid-for and without a loan. We have sown seeds for our jet also. We do this all the time whenever we foresee a need for something big in the future. Don't wait until you are desperate before you start to believe for your needs – remember that seeds take time to grow!

Once I have sown my financial seed and prayed in faith, I simply keep praising God until the harvest comes. The timing is none of my business! I keep serving God with the work He gives me to do and in time the miracles happen.

> *'And let us not be weary in well doing: for in due season we shall reap, if we faint not.'*   (Galatians 6:9)

Chapter 20

Warnings From the Word!

*'And it shall be, when the L*ORD *thy God shall have brought thee into the land which he sware unto thy fathers, to Abraham, to Isaac, and to Jacob, to give thee great and goodly cities, which thou buildedst not, And houses full of all good things, which thou filledst not, and wells digged, which thou diggedst not, vineyards and olive trees, which thou plantedst not; when thou shalt have eaten and be full;* **Then beware lest thou forget the L**ORD, *which brought thee forth out of the land of Egypt, from the house of bondage.'*

(Deuteronomy 6:10–12)

And later on it says:

'Therefore thou shalt keep the commandments of the LORD **thy God, to walk in his ways, and to fear him. For the L**ORD **thy God bringeth thee into a good land,** *a land of brooks of water, of fountains and depths that spring out of valleys and hills; A land of wheat, and barley, and vines, and fig trees, and pomegranates; a land of oil olive, and honey; A land wherein thou shalt eat bread without scarceness, thou shalt not lack any thing in it; a land whose stones are iron, and out of whose hills thou mayest dig brass. When thou hast eaten and art full, then thou shalt bless the L*ORD *thy God for the good land which he hath given thee.* **Beware that thou forget not the L**ORD **thy God, in not keeping his commandments, and his judgments, and his statutes,** *which I command thee this day:* **Lest when thou hast eaten and art full, and hast built goodly**

houses, and dwelt therein; *And when thy herds and thy flocks multiply, and thy silver and thy gold is multiplied, and all that thou hast is multiplied;* **Then thine heart be lifted up, and thou forget the** Lord **thy God,** *which brought thee forth out of the land of Egypt, from the house of bondage; Who led thee through that great and terrible wilderness, wherein were fiery serpents, and scorpions, and drought, where there was no water; who brought thee forth water out of the rock of flint; Who fed thee in the wilderness with manna, which thy fathers knew not, that he might humble thee, and that he might prove thee,* **to do thee good at thy latter end;** *And* **thou say in thine heart, My power and the might of mine hand hath gotten me this wealth.'**   (Deuteronomy 8:6–17)

All these Scriptures speak for themselves. They by no means teach that prosperity is wrong, but rather warn us **to guard our hearts** *as* **we prosper** to make sure that we keep our priorities in order and put our devotion to the Lord in first place.

It is interesting that when we are in need financially we tend to spend more time seeking God than in times of plenty. **But this should not be the case**! When we are in abundance we should be seeking God as to where we should give it. This must surely be a challenge to those who have an abundance. I find that as God blesses me more financially, He gives me correspondingly larger projects to concentrate on, which in turn causes me to continue seeking Him about my finances. This is definitely motivating!

'But thou shalt remember the Lord *thy God: for it is he that giveth thee power to get wealth, that he may establish his covenant which he sware unto thy fathers, as it is this day.'*   (Deuteronomy 8:18)

'Charge them that are rich in this world, that they be not highminded, nor trust in uncertain riches, but in the living God, who giveth us richly all things to enjoy; That they do good, that they be rich in good works, ready to distribute, willing to communicate; Laying up in store for

themselves a good foundation against the time to come, that they may lay hold on eternal life.'   (1 Timothy 6:17–19)

Both the Old and New Testament warn the people of God about not being covetous of material or other things. However, this does not stop us from believing God for the things that we need for this life. Covetousness means to lust after something that you do not have, or that belongs to someone else, as the following verses show:

'Thou shalt not covet thy neighbour's house, thou shalt not covet thy neighbour's wife, nor his manservant, nor his maidservant, nor his ox, nor his ass, nor any thing that is thy neighbour's.'   (Exodus 20:17)

'I have coveted no man's silver, or gold, or apparel.'
(Acts 20:33)

'For the love of money is the root of all evil: which while some coveted after, they have erred from the faith, and pierced themselves through with many sorrows.'
(1 Timothy 6:10)

It is interesting to note that when someone is in need materially they could be tempted to fall into covetousness because of their need. Conversely, someone who has everything they require may never be tempted to covet because they are content. However, there are others who are never satisfied by material things. As soon as they have one thing they want to change it for something else! The point I am making is that regardless of our financial circumstances, we may find ourselves having to guard against covetousness at some time or other. Another aspect to this is that just because we have never been attacked by covetousness so far does not mean that we never will be!

Jesus Himself tells this story;

*'And he said unto them, **Take heed, and beware of covetousness: for a man's life consisteth not in the abundance of the things which he possesseth.** And he spake a parable unto them, saying, The ground of a certain rich man brought forth plentifully: And he thought within himself, saying, What shall I do, because I have no room*

where to bestow my fruits? And he said, This will I do: I will pull down my barns, and build greater; and there will I bestow all my fruits and my goods. And I will say to my soul, Soul, thou hast much goods laid up for many years; take thine ease, eat, drink, and be merry. But God said unto him, Thou fool, this night thy soul shall be required of thee: then whose shall those things be, which thou hast provided? **So is he that layeth up treasure for himself, and is not rich toward God.**' (Luke 12:15–21)

Chapter 21

Increase and Prosperity
Everywhere

'And he said, So is the kingdom of God, as if a man should cast seed into the ground; And should sleep, and rise night and day, and the seed should spring and grow up, he knoweth not how. For the earth bringeth forth fruit of herself; first the blade, then the ear, after that the full corn in the ear.' (Mark 4:26–28)

This portion of Scripture shows that seeds often produce a harvest in stages rather than all at once. I would like to give you two instances where this has happened in my life recently, and where the Holy Spirit has prophetically used the above verses regarding financial situations. The first example is when I went to America a few years ago. Before I went the Lord spoke to my heart and told me to believe for a certain amount of money from this trip for the work of the ministry. I had asked in faith for £2000 and God told me to believe Him for £5000. I gulped but obeyed. I prayed in faith as the Spirit had led me.

During the first week of the trip, however, the offerings I received after having ministered were very low. At the end of the first week the Lord spoke to me again and said, *'First the blade, then the ear, after that the full corn in the ear'* and said that the harvest would come in three stages. During the second week I saw a major increase, which constituted the 'ear'. I was waiting for the 'full corn in the ear' during the last week and so was disappointed when I left the USA to come home, since the money I received came very short of the figure God had promised. However, the very day I arrived home I had a phone call from some people in California saying that they were going to pay the air fare for our whole family to go to America that summer for a holiday. That was the 'full corn in the ear'! When I calculated all that I had been given during those three weeks it came to £5000 almost to the pound!

This is not an isolated case with my mission trips, since God often speaks to me regarding finances and what He wants me to believe for in faith. Incidentally, I seek never to let people know what I am believing for or try to manipulate them to get them to give. If God sends me on a trip then He will provide the money without my having to advertise my needs or borrow. After visiting 29 countries in four years I can say that God has never failed me!

The other example involving Mark 4:28 is in another financial situation regarding the ministry. As I mentioned earlier, we were believing God for a building of our own since we were a young church renting a building each week and carrying our equipment in several cars to every meeting. We took up an offering and the Lord spoke to me immediately regarding sowing into another ministry's building fund since seeds produce after their own kind. We gave £700, which was a large gift for a young church.

About one year later we were offered our present building for one sixth of the usual lease cost. Our building is an absolute miracle and we praise God regularly for His grace. However, after we had been in it for only a few weeks, the Lord spoke to me so clearly and said, *'This building is **the blade!**'* I was so excited by that prophetic word to my heart. We are still waiting in faith for 'the ear' to manifest but I know it will come. In fact, I believe the 'full corn in the ear' for us as a ministry is the 5,000–seater building in the building complex I mentioned in chapter 19.

So we can see how prosperity and increase usually come in stages, and that we must wait patiently for each stage to come. Hasty Christians have found themselves in a lot of trouble by running ahead financially and trying to bite off

more than they can chew. This is not faith but presumption
– and we all have to guard against it!

Take a close look at the following Scriptures regarding
increase and prosperity and allow the Holy Spirit to reveal
the full truth of God's word about this subject:

*'I, even I, have spoken; yea, I have called him: I have
brought him, and he shall make his way prosperous.
Come ye near unto me, hear ye this; I have not spoken in
secret from the beginning; from the time that it was, there
am I: and now the Lord God, and his Spirit, hath sent me.
Thus saith the* Lord, *thy Redeemer, the Holy One of
Israel; I am the* Lord *thy God which teacheth thee to
profit, which leadeth thee by the way that thou
shouldest go.* O *that thou hadst hearkened to my
commandments! then had thy peace been as a river, and
thy righteousness as the waves of the sea.'*

(Isaiah 48:15–18)

*'Blessed is the man that walketh not in the counsel of
the ungodly, nor standeth in the way of sinners, nor
sitteth in the seat of the scornful. But his delight is in
the law of the* Lord; *and in his law doth he meditate
day and night. And he shall be like a tree planted by
the rivers of water, that bringeth forth his fruit in his
season; his leaf also shall not wither; and whatsoever
he doeth shall prosper.'* (Psalm 1:1–3)

*'Thou hast caused men to ride over our heads; we went
through fire and through water: but thou broughtest
us out into a wealthy place.'* (Psalm 66:12)

*'Blessed are they that dwell in thy house: they will be
still praising thee. Selah. Blessed is the man whose
strength is in thee; in whose heart are the ways of
them. Who passing through the valley of Baca make it a
well; the rain also filleth the pools. They go from strength to
strength, every one of them in Zion appeareth before God.'*

(Psalm 84:4–7)

'For the Lord *God is a sun and shield: the* Lord *will
give grace and glory: no good thing will he withhold*

> *from them that walk uprightly. O Lord of hosts,*
> *blessed is the man that trusteth in thee.'*
>
> (Psalm 84:11–12)

Note: the word *'blessed'* can equally be translated 'empowered to prosper'.

> *'The Lord shall increase you more and more, you and*
> *your children.'*   (Psalm 115:14)

I was recently speaking on the subject of contentment and I came across an amazing verse regarding financial prosperity:

> *'But godliness with contentment is great gain.'*
>
> (1 Timothy 6:6)

We certainly need to develop in both the vital areas of godliness and contentment. However, the phrase 'great gain' is very interesting if you examine the meaning in the original Greek. It comes from the word *'megas'*, meaning 'big, exceedingly great, high, large, loud, mighty, strong and furnishing or procuring financial gain or acquisition'.

Thus, if we expand this definition, we can translate 1 Timothy 6:6 like this:

> *'But godliness with contentment is **mega, exceeding,***
> ***mighty financial gain.'***

Therefore if we can maintain a godly life, seeking first His kingdom, feeding the poor, seeking to give and not to get, honouring God with our money at all times, being content materially and eliminating all covetousness, then we are scripturally entitled to lead a life of continual prosperity. This will enable us to serve God at all times with more than enough to bless all who come our way and see His work established and continually increasing. To God be all the glory!

Chapter 22

Grace and Favour in Prosperity

As believers we are God's chosen people as well as being His children. The Scriptures make it abundantly clear that we are therefore recipients of **His divine favour**. It is most interesting when you study the connection between grace, favour and prosperity in both the Old and the New Testaments that the Hebrew and Greek meanings for these words are strongly connected.

I have noticed on many occasions how often the Lord does things for me and gives me favour just because I am His child. I believe that I receive preferential treatment because God is on my side all the time. In fact, I am learning to expect His favour more and more in every area of life.

An interesting thing happened to our family very recently. Our son David has been learning the cello for many years but wanted to give it up so that he could spend more time on his studies. Ruth and I would have preferred him to continue but knew that he would only have been doing it under sufferance, so we decided to sell the cello. We had bought it about three years ago for £190 through a local newspaper advertisement. I did not know how much to sell it for so I made a few enquiries. The first dealer told me that it would sell for about £390. I was delighted and so I advertised it for that price. Then I spoke to another Christian dealer who informed me that it would sell for about £450. This was getting better all the time! I advertised it for £430 and sold it in a very short time. That is financial favour! The wealth of the sinner is laid up for the just. I used my common sense to find out about its value and God gave me tremendous favour. After we had tithed on the money, we were able to put it towards a new computer for the family – something for which we had been believing God already.

Expect favour in all the affairs of life. When you go for a job interview, take your driving test, sit your exams, book a holiday, or simply go to the supermarket you can believe for and expect the favour of God all the time. I do and it is so exciting to see time and time again how His favour blesses us continually.

In order to receive this favour, it is vital to understand and believe how special you are to God. If you do not know who you are in Christ then I suggest you order two of my books which will help you: *Secrets of Success* and *Angels, Demons and Spiritual Warfare* (our address is at the back of this book).

Divine favour in the Old Testament

Study the following verses and see how many times favour is mentioned.

> *'And he left all that he had in Joseph's hand; and he knew not ought he had, save the bread which he did eat. **And Joseph was a goodly person, and well favoured.**'*
>
> (Genesis 39:6)

> *'**But the Lord was with Joseph, and showed him mercy, and gave him favour in the sight of the keeper of the prison.**'*   (Genesis 39:21)

Throughout the life of Joseph we can see time and time again how God's favour just shone on him. Even when his circumstances were awful, the favour of God never ceased to work because his heart was right with the Lord and he did those things that were pleasing to God. Even in prison, where he was put after being falsely accused of adultery, he was given immediate favour.

We see the ultimate favour of God in the life of Joseph when he rode in the second chariot in the whole of Egypt after the Lord had made him a very wealthy man.

'And I will give this people favour in the sight of the Egyptians: and it shall come to pass, that, when ye go, ye shall not go empty.'   (Exodus 3:21)

'And **the LORD gave the people favour in the sight of the Egyptians.** *Moreover the man Moses was very great in the land of Egypt, in the sight of Pharaoh's servants, and in the sight of the people.'*   (Exodus 11:3)

'And **the LORD gave the people favour in the sight of the Egyptians,** *so that they lent unto them such things as they required.* **And they spoiled the Egyptians.'**

(Exodus 12:36)

Here we see once again the link between favour and prosperity because on the day that Israel left the bondage of Egypt they were given all sorts of riches by the Egyptians themselves!

'And Moses said unto the LORD, **Wherefore hast thou afflicted thy servant? and wherefore have I not found favour in thy sight,** *that thou layest the burden of all this people upon me?'*   (Numbers 11:11)

Moses was so used to seeing the favour of God in his life that he had come to expect it at all times – in this verse we see him asking God where His favour was. I really believe that we should be like that as God's blood-bought children. I treat my children with favour all the time and often look for different ways in which to bless them. How much more do you think our wonderful Father in Heaven will do for you when your life is totally submitted to His will?

'And Boaz answered and said unto her, It hath fully been showed me, all that thou hast done unto thy mother in law since the death of thine husband: and how thou hast left thy father and thy mother, and the land of thy nativity, and art come unto a people which thou knewest not heretofore. The LORD recompense thy work, and a full reward be given thee of the LORD God of Israel, under whose wings thou art come to trust. **Then she said, Let me find favour in thy sight, my lord;** *for that thou hast comforted me, and for that thou*

> *hast spoken friendly unto thine handmaid, though I be not like unto one of thine handmaidens.'*   (Ruth 2:11–13)

This is an awesome story about a young woman who was not even part of Israel and yet she expected favour from Boaz. Ruth must have begun to understand the ways of the Lord by spending time with God's people. Not only did Ruth find favour in the short term (all that she was hoping for at the time), she also became the **wife** of Boaz which made her into an extremely wealthy lady and also led to her becoming part of God's awesome plan of redemption. Ruth could never have realised that she would be the great-grandmother of king David and eventually an ancestor of the Lord Jesus Christ Himself! Now **that** is favour! Ruth was an outcast, a foreigner, a Moabite and very poor. She had no hope in the natural **but the favour of God brought her up from the lowest station in life up to the highest and most privileged place**. What a mighty God we serve! The favour of God can bring His children before kings and queens and presidents of nations, and open doors for the Gospel in ways that nothing else can.

> *'And **the child Samuel grew on, and was in favour both with the Lord, and also with men.'***   (1 Samuel 2:26)

Expect this kind of favour all the time both with the Lord and with men.

> *'Now when the turn of Esther, the daughter of Abihail the uncle of Mordecai, who had taken her for his daughter, was come to go in unto the king, she required nothing but what Hegai the king's chamberlain, the keeper of the women, appointed. And **Esther obtained favour in the sight of all them that looked upon her.'***   (Esther 2:15)

> *'**And the king loved Esther above all the women, and she obtained grace and favour in his sight more than all the virgins; so that he set the royal crown upon her head, and made her queen instead of Vashti.'***
>
> (Esther 2:17)

> *'And it was so, **when the king saw Esther the queen standing in the court, that she obtained favour in his***

sight: and the king held out to Esther the golden sceptre that was in his hand. So Esther drew near, and touched the top of the sceptre.' (Esther 5:2)

'If I have found favour in the sight of the king, and if it please the king to grant my petition, and to perform my request, let the king and Haman come to the banquet that I shall prepare for them, and I will do to morrow as the king hath said.' (Esther 5:8)

'Then Esther the queen answered and said, If I have found favour in thy sight, O king, and if it please the king, let my life be given me at my petition, and my people at my request.' (Esther 7:3)

It should be obvious to you now that the people of God had come to expect divine favour at all times and in all situations which promoted them above others, increased their financial blessing and gave them greater influence in the world.

'For thou, LORD, wilt bless the righteous; **with favour wilt thou compass him as with a shield.'** (Psalm 5:12)

'For his anger endureth but a moment; in his favour is life: weeping may endure for a night, but joy cometh in the morning.' (Psalm 30:5)

'LORD, by thy favour thou hast made my mountain to stand strong: thou didst hide thy face, and I was troubled.' (Psalm 30:7)

'Let them shout for joy, and be glad, that favour my righteous cause: yea, let them say continually, Let the LORD be magnified, which hath pleasure in the prosperity of his servant.' (Psalm 35:27)

This verse actually gives us a definite connection with both favour and prosperity. This verse ought to be on the lips of all believers to defend against a poverty spirit and to keep the devil at bay where finances are concerned. The favour of God is upon our righteous cause, which gives us confidence to pursue our goals and see the kingdom advancing continually.

*'**My son, forget not my law; but let thine heart keep my commandments**: For length of days, and long life, and peace, shall they add to thee. **Let not mercy and truth forsake thee: bind them about thy neck; write them upon the table of thine heart: So shalt thou find favour and good understanding in the sight of God and man.**'*

(Proverbs 3:1–4)

'For whoso findeth me findeth life, and shall obtain favour of the LORD.'   (Proverbs 8:35)

'Me' in the above verse is referring to Christ Jesus, who is our wisdom.

*'**He that diligently seeketh good procureth favour**: but he that seeketh mischief, it shall come unto him.'*

(Proverbs 11:27)

*'**A good man obtaineth favour of the LORD**: but a man of wicked devices will he condemn.'*   (Proverbs 12:2)

*'Fools make a mock at sin: **but among the righteous there is favour.**'*   (Proverbs 14:9)

An alternative meaning for *'grace'*

The word 'grace' appears many times in the New Testament in many different contexts. However, it can equally be translated as 'wealth', 'prosperity', 'favour', 'benefit' or 'liberality'.

You will notice that all of Paul's letters began and ended by proclaiming grace upon each church. Here are a few examples;

'The grace of our Lord Jesus Christ be with you all. Amen.'

(Romans 16:24)

'Grace be unto you, and peace, from God our Father, and from the Lord Jesus Christ. I thank my God always on your behalf, for the grace of God which is given you by Jesus Christ.'   (1 Corinthians 1:3–4)

'Elect according to the foreknowledge of God the Father, through sanctification of the Spirit, unto obedience and

sprinkling of the blood of Jesus Christ: Grace unto you, and peace, be multiplied.' (1 Peter 1:2)

'Of which salvation the prophets have inquired and searched diligently, who prophesied of the grace that should come unto you.' (1 Peter 1:10)

'Wherefore gird up the loins of your mind, be sober, and hope to the end for the grace that is to be brought unto you at the revelation of Jesus Christ.' (1 Peter 1:13)

'Grace and peace be multiplied unto you through the knowledge of God, and of Jesus our Lord.' (2 Peter 1:2)

'But grow in grace, and in the knowledge of our Lord and Saviour Jesus Christ. To him be glory both now and for ever. Amen.' (2 Peter 3:18)

Thus, favour should come to us in abundance and grow in every way. We should expect the divine favour of God to increase in our lives day by day as our revelation of God's love and provision for us grows. It is His will for us to prosper and receive His blessings. To God be the glory for evermore!

Other books by Trevor Newport

- *King Jesus is Coming Soon!*
- *Angels, Demons and Spiritual Warfare*
- *The Ministry of Jesus Christ*
- *Divine Appointments*
- *The Two Us: Unbelief and Unforgiveness*
- *Secrets of Success*
- *From Victory to Victory*
- *Pitfalls in Ministry*
- *How to Pray in the Spirit*

For more information about any aspect of this ministry please contact:

Life-Changing Ministries
Bemersley House
Gitana Street
Hanley
Stoke-on-Trent
Staffordshire
ST1 1DY
ENGLAND

Phone/Fax: 01782 272 671
(*overseas*: +44 1782 272 671)